Essentials of Sensation and Perception

The study of sensation and perception looks at how we acquire, process, and interpret information about the outside world. By describing key ideas from first principles, this straightforward introduction provides easy access to the basic concepts in the subject and incorporates the most recent advances with useful historical background. The text takes a uniquely integrative approach, highlighting fundamental findings that apply across all the senses – including vision, hearing, touch, pain, balance, smell, and taste – rather than considering each sense in isolation.

Several pedagogical features help students to engage with the material. 'Key Term' and 'Key Concept' boxes describe technical terms and concepts, while 'Research Question' boxes relate the material to everyday questions about perception. Each chapter ends with suggestions for further reading, and the final chapter draws together the material from the previous chapters, summarizing the broad principles described and outlining some major unresolved issues.

Assuming no prior knowledge, this book is an accessible and up-to-date overview of the processes of human sensation and perception. It is an ideal introduction for pre-undergraduate and first-year undergraduate students on courses in psychology, as well as neuroscience and biology.

Essentials of Sensation and Perception

George Mather

Routledge
Taylor & Francis Group

LONDON AND NEW YORK

First published 2011
by Routledge
27 Church Road, Hove, East Sussex, BN3 2FA

Simultaneously published in the USA and Canada
by Routledge
711 Third Avenue, New York, NY 10017

Routledge is an imprint of the Taylor & Francis Group, an informa business

British Library Cataloguing in Publication Data
A catalogue record for this book is available from the British Library

Library of Congress Cataloging-in-Publication Data
Mather, George.
  Essentials of sensation and perception / George Mather.
    p. cm.
  Includes bibliographical references and index.
  ISBN 978-0-415-61514-3 (hardcover)—ISBN 978-0-415-58181-3 (pbk.)
1. Senses and sensation.   2. Perception.   I. Title.
  BF233.M276 2011
  152.1—dc22

                                                        2010050312

ISBN: 978-0-415-61514-3 (hbk)
ISBN: 978-0-415-58181-3 (pbk)

Typeset in Arial and Frutiger by RefineCatch Limited, Bungay, Suffolk, UK
Cover design by Lisa Dynan

Printed and bound in Slovenia

In memory of Doreen and Arthur Mather, 1931–2009

Contents

List of figures

Series preface

The Foundations of Psychology series provides undergraduates and pre-undergraduates with appealing and useful books that will enable students to expand their knowledge of key areas in psychology. The books go beyond the detail and discussion provided by general introductory books but will still be accessible and appropriate for this level.

This series will bridge the gap between the general introductory psychology textbook that covers all the major topics, and the advanced topic-specific books which might be inaccessible to students who are studying such topics for the first time. The books will also be of use to advanced undergraduates and postgraduates looking for a quick, easy-to-use study guide. Each book has a contemporary focus and fits into one of three main categories including:

- Themes and Perspectives (such as Theoretical Approaches or Ethics)
- Specific Topics (such as Memory or Relationships)
- Applied Areas (such as Psychology and Crime).

Series editors

Cara Flanagan is an experienced academic author and freelance lecturer in Psychology.

Philip Banyard is a Reader in Psychology at Nottingham Trent University.

Published
Stevenson/Cultural Issues in Psychology
Banyard and Flanagan/Ethical Issues in Psychology

Forthcoming
Lund/Attention (due Fall 2011)

Preface

A great deal is known about human sensation and perception, enough to occupy many volumes of textbooks, and more is being discovered and published every day. So it is a daunting task to write an introductory book that adequately conveys the current breadth of knowledge in this exciting area of science. Most textbooks on sensation and perception assume that the reader has already mastered some relevant introductory material. They typically devote a separate chapter, or several chapters, to detailed coverage of each sensory modality (vision, hearing, balance, and so on). Few books step back from the detail and try to offer a broader introductory perspective on the human senses, aimed at readers who do not have the relevant background knowledge. My aim in writing this book is to offer such a perspective. The chapters are organized so as to introduce general principles that apply across all the modalities in a logical sequence. The first chapter, for example, discusses sensory reception in all the senses. Later chapters consider sensory pathways and cortical processing, coding principles across the senses, and so on. The material is aimed at readers who have had little or no previous exposure to these topics, so the book is suitable for those studying prior to a university degree as well as those in the first year of a degree.

Several features are designed to make the material easier to understand, to offer opportunities to review your understanding, and to suggest directions for further study in a dynamic, ever-evolving area of science. *Key Term* boxes define terms in the margin when they are first used. *Key Concept* boxes give more background detail on important general concepts such as 'The neuron', 'fMRI', and 'Bayes' theorem'. Each chapter ends with suggestions for *Further Reading* and a *Reflective Exercise* containing three questions to assess learning: a multiple-choice question probes your knowledge; a second question probes critical thinking; and a third question prompts consideration of practical applications or ethical implications. *Research Question* boxes highlight research that bears on questions that might occasionally occur in everyday life, such as why you cannot tickle yourself, and why some modes of transport cause travel sickness. A comprehensive bibliography is provided so that the interested reader can delve into primary sources if they wish.

The text has been improved considerably as a result of many helpful and insightful comments and suggestions by several readers including Cara Flanagan, Matthew Isaak, and G. Neil Martin. Any remaining faults or errors are, of course, entirely my responsibility.

George Mather, November 2010

Sensory receptors

1

What this chapter will teach you

- What is the difference between sensation and perception?

- How many different kinds of sensory receptor do humans possess?

- How can hair cells signal sound and body position?

- How are the chemical components of gases, liquids, and solids detected?

- How many different kinds of photoreceptor does the eye contain?

- What sensory receptors signal pain?

Introduction

How do you survive in an environment full of challenges, including other creatures (predators, prey, fellow humans) and physical hazards (precipices, water, rock-falls, to name but a few)? The first step is to acquire information about them, as rapidly and as accurately as possible. This is the task of the human sensory systems. The information can take many forms, such as tiny vibrations in air pressure from animal calls or sudden impacts, volatile chemical substances from food sources, and electromagnetic radiation from the sun. So the human senses are extremely versatile and exquisitely sensitive. Continuous sensory input is so important to us that individuals deprived of external stimulation become severely disoriented and report vivid hallucinations, delusions, and distortions of body image. Prisoners held in the dark report seeing lights that appear out of the darkness in strange shifting forms ('prisoner's cinema'). Similar hallucinations have been reported by pilots flying through the dark for several hours. Sensory deprivation is so unpleasant and disorienting that it has been a widely used procedure during the interrogation of prisoners for many years (see reviews in Zubek, 1964; Sireteanu *et al.*, 2008).

This book is an introduction to the science of human sensation and perception. Sensations are the elementary experiences evoked by sensory stimulation, such as the sourness of lemon juice, the loudness of a whistle, or the sharpness of a pin-prick. These primitive sensations combine to create perceptions of organized, meaningful objects and events. For example, while viewing a sports event on television the visual system *senses* the fleeting changes in color and lightness on the screen, and the auditory system *senses* the complex fluctuations in loudness, pitch, and timbre emanating from the audio speaker. You may be aware, for instance, of how green is the grass on the sports field. From this mass of sensations you construct elaborate *perceptions* of the event, the athletes, and their actions.

Later in the book you will read about how perceptions are constructed from sensations, but the first step in your exploration of sensation and perception is to understand how sensations arise initially. How many different kinds of physical phenomena in the environment can you sense? In other words, how many different sensory systems do you have? Most people would probably say 'five'. These are the senses defined by

Key Terms

Sensation. An elementary experience evoked by stimulation of a sense organ, such as brightness, loudness, or saltiness.

Perception. A complex, meaningful experience of an external event or object, created from a combination of many different sensations.

your visible external sense organs; seeing with the eyes, hearing with the ears, smelling with the nose, tasting with the mouth, and touching with the skin. There are in fact other, more rigorous ways to count the number of sensory systems that humans possess based on the characteristics of the **nervous system**, and none of them produces the answer five. The first way to answer the question is to examine the different specialized receptor systems that the body uses to detect sensory stimuli.

Transduction

The nervous system is basically a device for processing information. Some of this information comes from the brain's memory stores, and some of it comes from the external environment. In this sense the nervous system is much like a typical personal computer. The computer's brain, its central processing unit (CPU), processes data that are stored in its memory or entered by the user with a keyboard, mouse, or some other interface device. Information is passed between the computer's components using electrical signals that mostly travel along thin copper wires. When you press a key or click a mouse button, for instance, mechanical switch closure causes a small electrical signal to be sent from that component to the CPU, which then acts on the input to, say, display a specific character on the screen. The nervous system also passes information between its components using electrical signals, which are generated by special brain cells called neurons.

However, in the case of the nervous system the process that initiates a signal about the external environment is much more complicated than a simple switch closure. Physical phenomena in the external environment can take many forms, as you read earlier: electromagnetic energy, air pressure fluctuation, volatile chemicals, mechanical force from contact with an external agent or object. All of these phenomena offer information that may have a bearing on wellbeing and survival, whether in identifying a food source or as an early warning of danger. In order to make use of this information, whatever form it takes, the system must convert it into an electrical signal that can be processed and interpreted by the brain. The brain must be able to infer the character of the external event from the signal, such as the particular spatial distribution of a light pattern, the direction of a

Key Terms

Transduction. The conversion of environmental energy into neural signals by sensory receptor cells.

Sensory receptor. A specialized nerve cell that transduces environmental energy into an electrical signal.

sudden impact, the chemical composition of a volatile substance, or the level of threat offered by a mechanical force. The process of converting external energy into electrical nerve impulses is called **transduction**, and it is achieved by a specialized class of neuron called **sensory receptors**. Clearly

KEY CONCEPT

Neuron

Brain cells come in two types, neurons and glial cells. Neurons (also called nerve cells) are specialized for sending electrical signals, while glial cells provide support and maintenance for neurons. The main components of a neuron, shown in Figure 1.1, are the cell body, dendrites, and axon. The cell body contains the nerve cell's DNA, and is responsible for making energy and disposing of waste. The dendrites have a branched tree-like structure, and receive electrical signals from other neurons. The axon (sometimes called a nerve fiber) forms a long, fine filament. Its job is to carry the neuron's own electrical signal from the cell body to the terminals at the end of the axon, which transmit the signal to the dendrites of other neurons. The signals themselves are brief electrical impulses or 'action potentials' (also called spikes) that propagate along axons rather like a spark traveling along a lit fuse.

The junctions between the axon terminals of one cell and dendrites of another are called synapses. When an action potential arrives at the axon's terminals it causes special chemicals called neurotransmitters to be released across the synapse. These transmitters can excite a neighboring cell or inhibit it, and the likelihood that a cell will produce its own action potential depends on the relative amount of excitatory and inhibitory signals it receives from other cells at its dendrites. Axons can carry signals over great distances. The axons that send signals from your toes to the spinal cord can be over a meter long (in a whale they can be 20 meters long). The speed of electrical transmission along axons is approximately 30 meters per second, vastly slower than the transmission of signals in the copper circuits of your computer. So it can take nearly a tenth of a second for the signal from your stubbed toe to reach your brain (depending on how tall you are). The hugely complex pattern of synaptic connections made by neurons in your brain governs your thought patterns and cognitive abilities.

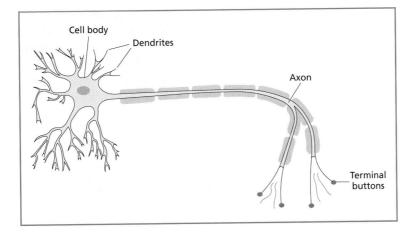

Figure 1.1 The main components of a neuron. The cell body contains the cell's DNA, and manages energy resources; the dendrites receive signals from other cells; the axon propagates an electrical signal to the cell's terminal buttons, where they make contact with the dendrites of other cells.

different forms of external energy require different kinds of sensory receptor. The human sensory systems possess just four different kinds of sensory receptor, known as mechanoreceptors, chemoreceptors, photoreceptors, and nociceptors.

Classes of sensory receptor

Mechanoreceptors

This form of sensory receptor responds to mechanical distortion by producing an electrical impulse. It is the most ubiquitous and versatile of all the sensory receptors, and mediates your perception of sound, touch, balance, body position, and body movement. Mechanoreceptors are sensitive to stretching in some part of the cell's structure, and typically produce electrical impulses at a rate that reflects the character of the mechanical stimulus.

Stretch sensitivity is ancient, and is found in the most ancient and primitive organisms such as bacteria. In humans a variety of specialized sensory cells underneath the skin respond to mechanical stimulation; some respond best to fluctuations in pressure level, and others respond best to steady pressure. The Pacinian corpuscle illustrated in Figure 1.2, for example, lies deep within the skin and can be up to 2 mm long. It has an onion-like capsule and is

Figure 1.2 A Pacinian corpuscle. The onion-like capsule is formed from concentric layers of collagen fibers separated by fluid. Action potentials travel down the nerve fiber.

capable of producing action potentials at a very high rate (over 300 impulses per second) when subjected to rapid mechanical stimulation, such as when a hand is drawn across a finely textured surface.

Stretch receptors deep in the body signal the state of tension in the musculature, and the disposition and movement of the limbs. Receptors inside the muscles signal the length of the muscle as it is stretched, while receptors in the tendons that attach the muscle to the bone signal how hard the muscle is pulling.

In another form of mechanoreceptor, the hair cell, tiny hair-like filaments protrude into a fluid-filled chamber or canal (see Figure 1.3). The cell produces action potentials when the hairs are deflected by movement of the fluid. This type of cell produces a moderate number of neural discharges even in the absence of stimulation, which allows the cell to signal the direction of fluid movement by the direction of change in activity level. Flow in one direction increases the cell's activity, and flow in the opposite direction decreases the cell's activity. This kind of mechanically driven response mediates your senses of both hearing and body position.

Body position and movement are sensed in the **vestibular labyrinths** or **organs**, located on either side of the head inboard of the ears. Each labyrinth is a complicated structure comprising three ring-shaped canals (**semi-circular canals**) and two

Key Terms

Vestibular labyrinths/organs. Bony, fluid-filled structures buried deep in the temporal bone of the head, which house the receptors that signal head position and movement.

Semi-circular canals. Three ring-shaped canals in each vestibular organ, arranged approximately at right-angles to each other; they contain receptors that signal angular acceleration of the head.

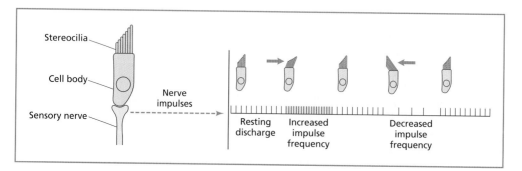

Figure 1.3 In a hair cell (left) tiny hair-like filaments called stereocilia protrude into fluid. Movement of the fluid towards the tallest hairs increases the firing rate of the cell, while movement in the opposite direction decreases the firing of the cell (right).

chambers (called the **saccule** and the **utricle**; see Figure 1.4). Each canal and chamber is filled with fluid, and contains a patch of hair cells. Rapid head-turns are sensed by a clump of hair cells (**crista**) in each of three semi-circular canals. As the head begins to rotate, the fluid in one or more of the canals lags behind momentarily because of inertia, causing a backward deflection of the crista. The resulting increase or decrease in neural discharge signals the direction of head rotation. Static head tilt is sensed by hair cells in the two chambers. The fluid above the hair cells contains

Key Terms

Saccule and **utricle**. Two chambers in the vestibular organ which contain receptors that signal head tilt and linear acceleration.

Crista. A patch of sensory hair cells in a swelling (ampulla) of each semi-circular canal.

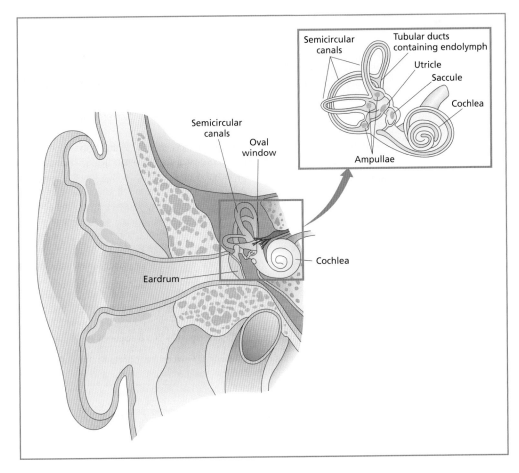

Figure 1.4 The vestibular system.

crystals that shift under gravity as the head tilts, in the same way that a loose hat wobbles to one side as you tilt your head. The wobble deflects the hair cells underneath, so signaling head tilt. Each labyrinth is exquisitely designed to detect movement or tilt in any direction, by virtue of the different angles of its component parts. The mechanism is, unfortunately, prone to disruption. When one comes to a stop after a rapid pirouette the fluid in the canals continues to spin for a short time, so the crista is deflected forward, signaling body rotation in the opposite direction to the original spin. The resulting disorientation and illusion of movement (dizziness) form what is called the oculogyral illusion (Graybiel & Hupp, 1946). Ingestion of alcohol causes the crista to become slightly buoyant because the alcohol in circulating blood is relatively light. Buoyancy causes the crista to wobble slightly, creating the dizziness and gaze instability associated with alcohol intoxication (Money & Myles, 1974).

KEY CONCEPT

Sound

A vibrating surface displaces the air surrounding it, pushing the air molecules to and fro. The repetitive increases (compression) and decreases (rarefaction) in air pressure generate a pressure wave that travels through the air quite slowly, at roughly 335 meters per second. If you could see this pressure wave it would look like the ripples that you see when a pebble drops into a pond. Instead, you hear it as sound. Closely spaced ripples or waves alternate between compression and rarefaction rapidly or at high frequency, and correspond perceptually to high-pitched sounds. Widely spaced waves make low frequency or low-pitched sounds. Sound frequency is measured in terms of the number of cycles between compression and rarefaction that occur in every second, cycles per second or hertz (Hz). Humans can hear sounds with frequencies between about 20 Hz and 20,000 Hz. Human voices generally contain frequencies between 120 Hz and 2000 Hz. In music, middle C corresponds to a frequency of 440 Hz.

The peak-to-trough height of a sound wave corresponds to the maximum change in pressure generated by the pressure wave, and defines the amplitude of the sound, normally heard as its loudness.

Notice that all sounds need air, so there is no sound in a vacuum. 'In space, no one can hear you scream' (*Alien*; Carroll & Scott, 1979) was an accurate tag-line. Space-ship engines can make no noise in space, despite what you might hear in the movies.

Sounds are sensed by hair cells in the cochlea, which sits right next to the vestibular organ (see Figure 1.4). The cochlea is a long, fluid-filled tube wrapped into a spiral about 10 mm in diameter. Hair cells are spread along a thin membrane known as the basilar membrane, which runs along the middle of the cochlea. Sound vibrations on each eardrum are transmitted by three tiny bones to a small window at the end of the tube, where they set up waves in the fluid that displace the basilar membrane and activate the hair cells (see Figure 1.5). The waves fluctuate rapidly in synchrony with the sound vibration, causing synchronous fluctuations in hair cell activity (recall from earlier that hair cells respond differentially to opposite directions of displacement). So the frequency of fluctuations in hair cell activity signals the frequency or pitch of the sound wave. Because of the mechanical properties of the basilar membrane, high frequency sounds cause maximum displacement near the base of the cochlea, while low frequency sounds cause more extensive displacement nearer the apex of the cochlea (see Moore, 1997). This offers a second potential code for the frequency of the sound wave, namely the place of maximum hair-cell activation along the basilar membrane. The coiled shape of the cochlea minimizes the space it occupies in the head while maximizing blood and nerve supply, as well as enhancing its response to low-pitched sounds (Manoussaki et al., 2008).

Cochlear hair cells are amazingly sensitive. They can respond to hair displacements as small as 0.3 nanometers (less than a billionth of a meter), which is shorter than the wavelength of visible light. Transduction can occur over a time period as short as 10 microseconds (millionths of a second; Hudspeth, 1989).

Key Terms

Cochlea. A spiral-shaped organ in the inner ear, where sound vibrations are transduced into electrical signals.

Basilar membrane. A flexible partition running along the length of the cochlea, which houses the mechanoreceptors that transduce sound energy into electrical signals.

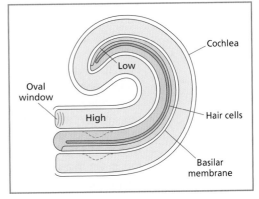

Figure 1.5 Transduction of sound by the cochlea. Sound vibrations arriving at the oval window cause ripples in the cochlear fluid that displace the basilar membrane and stimulate its hair cells. High frequency sounds mostly excite cells near the base, while low frequency sounds are more effective near the apex.

Chemoreceptors

Survival depends on your ability to discriminate between edible and inedible substances, and to avoid contact with harmful substances that might cause disease or infection. Chemoreceptors give you the ability to analyze the chemical composition of thousands of gases, liquids, and solids. You have two kinds of chemoreceptor: gustatory chemoreceptors are found in the mouth, mostly on the tongue. Olfactory chemoreceptors are found in the nose, high up in the nasal cavity, and in the throat.

Gustatory receptors are grouped together in taste bud cells. There is a continual turnover in taste bud receptor cells, which have a very short life span of up to about three weeks. There are five types of taste receptor cell selectively responsive to one of five classes of chemical compound, namely sugars, salts, acids, plant alkaloids, and amino acids. The first four of these receptor types map neatly onto the four basic perceptual taste qualities that psychologists had identified 120 years ago, namely sweetness, saltiness, sourness, and bitterness. The fifth taste receptor type is called the 'umami' receptor (after the Japanese word for 'yummy'). It responds to monosodium glutamate (MSG), and mediates your perception of savoriness, such as you might sense in a meaty broth (Beauchamp, 2009). The five receptor types relay useful information about potential foods. Sweetness identifies energy-rich nutritious food, while saltiness identifies food that can replace salts lost by sweating or bleeding (salt is essential for proper neural function). MSG content is useful for identifying high-protein foods. Sourness and bitterness warn against the ingestion of potentially noxious and poisonous chemicals, often produced by decomposition. The attractiveness of MSG has not been lost on food manufacturers, who add it to food in order to enhance its savoriness.

Taste preferences do vary to some extent between species, and this can be linked to differences in the genes that code taste receptors. Cats avoid substances that taste sour or bitter to humans, and show a preference for certain amino acids, but they are completely indifferent to sweet-tasting substances. Recordings from nerve fibers and genetic studies of taste receptors have revealed that all cats lack a receptor for sweetness (Li et al., 2006). This may help to explain their strict carnivorous diet (unlike, say, dogs which do have a sweet receptor). Taste preferences are labile to some extent; preference for salty and sweet foods can be conditioned by experience during infancy (Beauchamp & Moran, 1982).

Most olfactory receptors are located in a small patch of tissue about the size of a postage stamp, high up in the roof of the nasal cavity. Small hair-like protrusions from each cell pick up chemicals that have wafted into the nose and dissolved in the olfactory mucus. Molecules in the receptors bind to the chemicals that make up odors. Each receptor acts as a molecule counter for a particular kind of chemical, and humans possess several hundred different receptor types (Firestein, 2001).

Roughly 1000 genes are devoted to olfactory receptors, but in humans over half of these are so-called pseudogenes that are not expressed in a functional receptor, which suggests that olfaction became less important during human evolution, leaving behind redundant genes. Nevertheless, the hundreds of different olfactory receptor types that are retained by humans permit us to discriminate thousands of different smells. The molecules in each odorous compound activate a number of different olfactory receptors. Conversely any one receptor type can respond to many different odors, as illustrated in Figure 1.6. This allows a relatively small number of different receptor types to mediate perception of a very large number of odors (Malnic *et al.*, 1999).

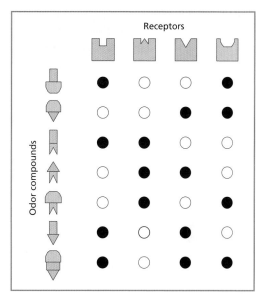

Figure 1.6 Coding of odor by olfactory receptors. Each receptor (top) responds to a specific chemical component of the odor (shapes at the top). Odor compounds (left-hand column) therefore excite several different receptors. Different compounds activate different combinations of receptor.

Photoreceptors

Electromagnetic energy from the sun is the power source for all life on earth. It travels in straight lines or rays at extremely high speed. A small portion of this energy is capable of producing a response in a special class of sensory receptor called photoreceptors, and you experience this sensation as light. When light strikes a surface it is either absorbed into the material (perhaps heating it up), reflected from it at a predictable angle (as in mirror reflections), or transmitted through it with a shift in direction (such as light refraction as it travels through glass). Photoreceptors line the inside surface of the eye to form part of the **retina**, and optical apparatus similar to that found in a camera admits light through the **pupil** and focuses it on the retina using a lens system (**cornea** and **lens**). The image formed on the retina carries a great deal of useful information about the immediate visual environment (see Figure 1.7).

Photoreceptors are capable of responding only to photon frequencies that have a wavelength within a relatively narrow range of

Key Terms

Retina. A network of cells lining the inside of the eye, containing the photoreceptors that transduce light energy into electrical signals.

Pupil. The circular aperture lying between the cornea and the lens, which regulates the amount of light entering the eye.

Cornea. The curved, transparent membrane through which light enters the eye.

Lens. A transparent object with a curved surface, which bends light passing through it to create an image on a suitably positioned surface placed behind it.

KEY CONCEPT

Light

Light is a form of energy known as electromagnetic radiation that travels between bodies at a constant but extremely high speed. The exact physical nature of light has puzzled philosophers and scientists throughout history, and is still not completely understood. Electromagnetic energy is known to travel in small packets called photons. The magnetic and electrical field of each photon has a characteristic oscillation frequency. You saw earlier in the case of sound waves that oscillation frequency is measured in cycles per second or hertz (Hz). The oscillation frequency of electromagnetic energy can vary from a few thousand cycles per second to many billions of cycles per second. This full range of frequencies is called the electromagnetic spectrum. Oscillation frequency can also be measured in terms of the distance between adjacent peaks in the wave, known as wavelength. When electromagnetic energy is expressed in terms of wavelength, it can vary from extremely short wavelengths that are a fraction of the size of atoms (X-rays and gamma rays, corresponding to the highest frequencies) to very long wavelengths that can be many kilometers long (the lower frequencies, used for telecommunications signals). The energy contained in each photon varies with frequency; gamma rays and X-rays are highly penetrating and destructive because they carry so much energy.

The energy that you can see, and call 'light', spans a tiny proportion of the full electromagnetic spectrum corresponding to wavelengths between 400 and 700 nanometers (billionths of a meter). Energy in this band is well-behaved, in the sense that it can be focused by lenses, and reflected off surfaces. The sense organ for vision, the eye, takes advantage of this good behavior.

between 400 and 700 nanometers, and this defines the visible spectrum of light. Pigments in the photoreceptors absorb light energy and convert it into neural signals. Each photoreceptor consists of an outer segment and an inner segment (Figure 1.8). The outer segment is arranged as a stack of disks containing light-sensitive pigment molecules (photopigments). The inner segment includes the cell nucleus and the terminals or synaptic clefts that make contact with adjacent cells.

As can be seen in Figure 1.8, human photoreceptors fall into two classes, called rods and cones on the basis of the shape

Key Terms

Rod. A type of photoreceptor that is specialized for responding in dim illumination.

Cone. A type of photoreceptor that is specialized for responding in bright illumination.

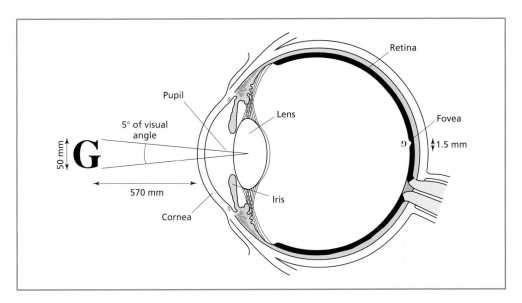

Figure 1.7 Image formation in the human eye. Light from an object passes through the cornea, pupil, and lens, and then forms an image on the retina. The image of a letter in a newspaper headline at reading distance is approximately 1.5 mm tall, spread over 500 receptors.

of their outer segment. Rods and cones differ in a number of ways that are all important for vision. The first major difference is that they respond to different ranges of light wavelength. As Figure 1.9 shows, all rods respond maximally to medium wavelength light, peaking at around 498 nm. Cones subdivide into three classes that respond over different wavelength ranges. 'Blue' cones peak at very short wavelengths around 420 nm in the blue part of the spectrum, 'green' cones peak at medium wavelengths around 534 nm, and 'red' cones peak at long wavelengths around 563 nm in the red region of the spectrum. Remarkable recent research has been able to measure the distribution of the different cone types across the living human retina using sophisticated photographic techniques. Hofer *et al.* (2005) found that on average only about 6% of

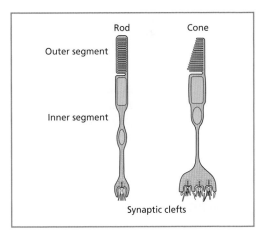

Figure 1.8 Photoreceptors. The outer segment contains light-sensitive pigment molecules; the inner segment includes the cell nucleus and terminals that connect to other cells (synaptic clefts).

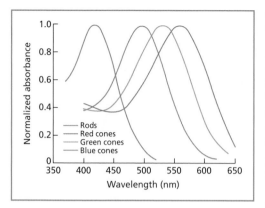

Figure 1.9 Absorbance spectra of human photoreceptors: Rods (peak: 498 nm); 'blue' cones (peak: 420 nm); 'green' cones (peak: 534 nm); and 'red' cones (peak: 563 nm). Data from Dartnall, Bowmaker, and Mollon (1983).

cones are of the 'blue' type, while 34% are 'green' cones, and 59% are 'red' cones. Interestingly there were huge differences between the eyes of different individuals, particularly in the relative proportions of red and green cones. The ratio of red to green cones varied from 1.1:1 to 16.5:1 for different individuals. Remarkably, despite this variation the different individuals produced normal scores on all tests of color vision.

The second important difference between rods and cones is that they operate over different ranges of light intensity. Rods are up to 100 times more sensitive to light than cones. Third, they differ in their relative number and distribution on the retina. Cones are packed tightly into the area of retina dealing with central vision, where you look, known as the **fovea**. Rods avoid the central retina entirely and are most numerous out in the periphery of your vision. There are about twenty times more rods in the retina than cones.

What do these differences between rods and cones mean for the sense of vision? During daylight vision is mediated by cones. The different classes of cone allow humans to detect variations in wavelength, which we perceive as color, and their close packing gives us high acuity for spatial detail. In evolutionary terms rods are a recent addition to the retina that allow us to sustain some visual sensation during the hours of darkness, but in the absence of color experience (because rods cannot distinguish different wavelengths). During darkness the light arriving at earth from stars is so weak that many seconds can elapse between successive photon strikes yet, amazingly, rods can produce a response even when struck by a single photon. However rod vision is very blurred and indistinct, partly because photons are so scarce and partly because rods are not packed together on the retina so tightly.

A number of perceptual deficiencies can be attributed to photoreceptors. Color blindness, for instance, is caused by an abnormality in the wavelength response of cones that impairs an individual's ability to discriminate colors (a more accurate term

Key Term

Fovea. A small area at the center of the retina, containing many densely packed cone photoreceptors but no rods.

is 'deficiency' rather than 'blindness'). Most commonly the sensitivity curves of the red and green cones (shown in Figure 1.9) are shifted closer together. The result is an impaired ability to discriminate between colors; about one in twelve people (mostly men) tend to confuse crimsons with blues, or scarlets with greens. More rarely there is a complete absence of one cone type, making it impossible to distinguish red from green.

RESEARCH QUESTION

Why do your pupils vary in size?

The obvious answer to this question is that the pupil varies in size in order to regulate the amount of light entering the eye. In bright conditions it is relatively small, and in darkness it is relatively large. But this answer is incomplete, and not entirely accurate. Human vision can function across a huge range of light levels; light reflected from a sheet of paper viewed in sunlight is over ten million times more intense than the light reflected from the same sheet of paper in moonlight. Yet pupil diameter can vary between approximately 2 mm and 8 mm, creating a sixteen-fold variation in light intensity entering the eye.

Research has shown that pupil size varies markedly with cognitive and emotional state. For example, Bradley *et al.* (2008) showed participants emotionally arousing or neutral images, and monitored change in pupil diameter after the appearance of each image. They found an initial decrease in diameter that was strongly related to light intensity, followed by increases in pupil diameter that were larger when the participants viewed arousing images (either pleasant or unpleasant) than when they viewed neutral images. Steinhauer *et al.* (2004) also found increases in pupil diameter while participants performed a difficult mental arithmetic task, compared to relatively easy control tasks.

In the movie *Blade Runner* (1982) changes in pupil size were used as a way to expose androids posing as humans, because only humans betrayed their emotions in their pupils. This particular piece of science fiction was based on some sound science.

Nociceptors

There are sensory neurons throughout the body that do not terminate in a specialized receptor, but have only a 'free nerve ending'. They can be found, for example, in the oral and nasal cavities, in the eyes, and in the skin. Chemicals, heat, or tissue damage either to the nerve ending itself or to the surrounding tissue provokes activation of these cells. They are relatively insensitive to stimulation, and only respond when the stimulus is dangerously intense. Their activation is associated with sensations of discomfort or pain, so they are called nociceptors ('noci' means 'hurt' in Latin; they do not actually detect pain as such, they detect tissue damage). The sensation of pain is associated with cortical processing, not with the sensory signals themselves. In a similar fashion, photoreceptors respond to light wavelengths; they do not detect color.

Nociceptors mediate everyday sensations such as the tingle of certain smells and tastes, the sting of soap in the eyes, the tiredness of muscles, and the sting of lemon juice on broken skin. There are at least two types of nociceptor fiber (Torebjork & Ochoa, 1990). One type, called Aδ fibers, seems to supply signals associated with the initial, rapid sensation of sharp pain. The other type, called C fibers, follows on with a slower, dull burning pain. C fibers are also associated with the burning sensation produced by capsaicin, the source of 'heat' in chilli peppers. These nociceptors are found all over the body, so chilli peppers can be felt in many other places, such as in the eyes if rubbed after chopping chilli peppers.

> ## DISCUSS AND DEBATE
>
> You can demonstrate the relatively slow transmission of signals along nociceptor fibers compared to mechanoreceptor fibers by allowing a drop of hot water to fall onto your hand. Notice that the contact of the water drop on the hand can be sensed about half a second before its temperature.

The importance of pain sensation for normal functioning is dramatically illustrated by rare cases of individuals who are incapable of feeling pain because of a congenital lack of Aδ and C fibers (Nagasako et al., 2003). Such individuals often die in childhood because they fail to notice illnesses and injuries such as painless burns, finger and toe mutilation, and joint damage.

Evaluation

By far the most numerous of all receptors are photoreceptors. Each eye contains a huge number of them, approximately 120 million rods and 6 million cones. At the other extreme, each cochlea possesses only 3500 sensory hair cells. In between these extremes lie chemoreceptors and other mechanoreceptors. There are roughly 6 million olfactory receptors in each nostril and 1 million gustatory receptors in the mouth. Each vestibular organ houses tens of thousands of hair cells, and there are perhaps 100,000 or more skin mechanoreceptors and nociceptors.

Humans are evidently highly visual creatures, but the inequalities in receptor populations may at least partly reflect the different coding requirements in different sensory modalities. Let's take the two extremes in terms of receptor counts, vision, and hearing. The visual image formed in the human eye extends over a very large area inside the eye (about 4.6 cm in diameter), and requires a correspondingly large two-dimensional array or matrix of photoreceptors packed sufficiently tightly to resolve some detail in the image (similarly a digital camera needs millions of 'pixels' to record a reasonable photographic image). Sound pressure waves arriving at each ear extend over one dimension of time rather than two of space, so receptors (and later processes) need high temporal resolution rather than dense two-dimensional spatial sampling. This fundamental difference between visual and auditory signals may help to explain why there are over thirty thousand times more photoreceptors than cochlear hair cells.

A detailed consideration of the four classes of sensory receptor captures some fundamentally important characteristics of human sensory systems. The diverse methods of transduction used in different sensory modalities are ingenious and amazingly sensitive. On the basis of receptor classes one might be tempted to conclude that humans possess four sensory systems, but a count based on receptor classes is not a very meaningful way to enumerate the systems as a substrate for sensory perception. For instance, although hearing and balance use very similar mechanoreceptors, they provide completely different kinds of information, and it is not sensible to consider them as a single system. A world in which sounds were confused with head turns would be a very strange world indeed. In order to make more sense of the sensory systems, it is essential to look at what happens to the neural signals once they leave the receptors, in the next chapter.

Summary

- Sensory information about the environment is vital for survival. Deprivation of sensory input leads to severe disorientation and hallucinations.
- The human sensory systems possess four kinds of receptor: mechanoreceptors, chemoreceptors, photoreceptors, and nociceptors.
- Mechanoreceptors respond to mechanical deformation, and are found all over the body. They detect sound, body position, body movement, and bodily touch. Stretch receptors in the body detect touch, position, and movement. Hair cells in the inner ear detect sounds, head position, and head movement.
- Chemoreceptors respond to the chemical components of gases, liquids, and solids. Olfactory chemoreceptors are found in the nose, and respond to chemical compounds in gases. Humans possess several hundred types of olfactory receptor. Gustatory chemoreceptors are found in the mouth, and respond to five kinds of chemical in liquids and solids: sugars, salts, acids, plant alkaloids, and amino acids.
- Photoreceptors respond to light. They form part of a network of cells lining the inside of the eye. Rod photoreceptors respond in dim light, and cone photoreceptors respond in bright light. There are far more rods in each eye than cones, but cones are subdivided into three types according to the light wavelengths that they can detect.
- Nociceptors do not have specialized sensory endings, but sense dangerously intense stimulation that is likely to cause tissue damage. They are found all over the body.

REFLECTIVE EXERCISE

1. Which of the following is not a class of human sensory receptor?
   a. Mechanoreceptor
   b. Photoreceptor
   c. Waveceptor
   d. Nociceptor

2. How would you design an experiment to test the idea that humans have a 'sixth sense' for direction based on receptors that sense the earth's magnetic field (as some birds have)?

3. Evaluate whether it is acceptable to add MSG to foodstuffs.

FURTHER READING

- Beauchamp, G.K. (2009) Sensory and receptor responses to umami: an overview of pioneering work. *American Journal of Clinical Nutrition*, *90* (Suppl), 723S–727S.
- Chandrashekar, J., Hoon, M.A., Ryba, N.J., & Zuker, C.S. (2006) The receptors and cells for mammalian taste. *Nature*, *444*, 288–294.
- Colclasure, J.C., & Holt, J.R. (2003) Transduction and adaptation in sensory hair cells of the mammalian vestibular system. *Gravitational and Space Biology Bulletin*, *16* (2), 61–70.
- Fildes, B.N., O'Loughlin, J., & Bradshaw, J.L. (1984) Human orientation with restricted sensory information: no evidence for magnetic sensitivity. *Perception*, *13*, 229–236.
- Hudspeth, A.J. (1989) How the ear's works work. *Nature*, *341*, 397–404.
- Masland, R.H. (2001) The fundamental plan of the retina. *Nature Neuroscience*, *4*, 877–886.
- Schnapf, J., & Baylor, D. (1987) How photoreceptor cells respond to light. *Scientific American*, *256* (4), 32–39.

Sensory pathways and cortical processing

2

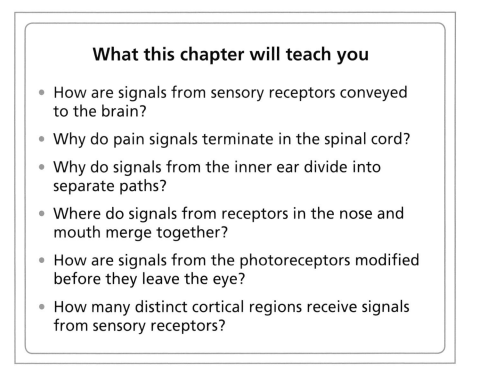

What this chapter will teach you

- How are signals from sensory receptors conveyed to the brain?

- Why do pain signals terminate in the spinal cord?

- Why do signals from the inner ear divide into separate paths?

- Where do signals from receptors in the nose and mouth merge together?

- How are signals from the photoreceptors modified before they leave the eye?

- How many distinct cortical regions receive signals from sensory receptors?

Introduction

You use **mechanoreceptor** signals to hear sounds, to keep your balance, and to stabilize your gaze, among other things. How can similar sensory receptors, producing identical trains of neural impulses, support such contrasting sensory and motor functions? The character and usefulness of a sensation are determined not by the type of receptor that initiated it, nor by the nature of the electrical impulses traveling to the brain, but by the routes those impulses take and their final destination. Much of this knowledge about the sensory pathways comes from neuroanatomy.

In 1888 the Spanish neuroanatomist Santiago Ramon y Cajal at the University of Barcelona was the first researcher to recognize that neurons were discrete entities that communicate with each other at junctions that are now called **synapses**. He used a staining technique that picked out individual neurons in anatomical tissue preparations. Cajal won the Nobel Prize for his neuron theory in 1906 (jointly with Camillo Golgi, who had discovered the staining technique). More recent neuroanatomical staining and tracing techniques have been used to map out in detail the various routes that the fibers of sensory neurons take on the way to the brain.

Sensory pathways

The fibers carrying receptor signals are bundled together into sensory nerves. Each nerve can contain thousands of individual fibers, rather like the many individual wires inside a large computer data cable. The optic nerve, for instance, contains about one million individual fibers. The length of the nerve and the route it takes to the brain vary for different groups of sensory receptors.

In all senses the final destination for incoming signals is the **cerebral cortex** in the brain. En route from the receptor cells to the cortex, sensory signals pass from one neuron to another at a series of synapses in various subcortical structures. These junctions are crucial points in the flow of sensory information because they allow the incoming information to be modulated and modified, and may incorporate branches that send the information

Key Terms

Mechanoreceptor. A class of sensory receptor cell that responds to mechanical distortion or deflection, such as a hair cell in the ear.

Synapse. A junction between two neurons where chemical signals pass from one neuron to the other.

Cerebral cortex. A thin, densely folded sheet of neurons covering the brain; although it is only 3 mm thick, the cerebral cortex has a total surface area of over two square meters, and contains about 10 billion brain cells.

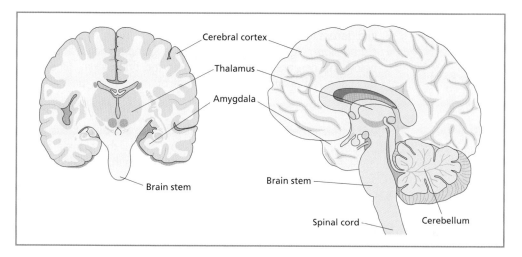

Figure 2.1 The main structures in the central nervous system that receive projections from the peripheral sense organs. The left-hand figure is a side-to-side (transverse) section through the middle of the brain. The right-hand figure is a front-to-back (sagittal) section through the middle of the brain.

to multiple destinations. Figure 2.1 illustrates the major structures in the central nervous system that contain synapses in the sensory pathways. These include the following:

- *Spinal cord*   A long thin tube of nervous tissue that runs up the middle of the backbone. It contains both afferent (incoming) sensory neurons that send signals to the brain, and efferent (outgoing) motor neurons that send signals to the muscles.
- *Brain stem*   The lower part of the brain, which sits on top of the spinal cord. Massive bundles of cells in the brain stem control functions such as arousal, alertness, and sleep.
- *Thalamus*   Several large masses of cell bodies sitting in the middle of the brain above the brain stem, about the size of a grape. They play a crucial role in regulating the flow of information into and out of the cerebral cortex. The thalamus acts as a sensory relay station, and also seems to act as the gatekeeper for consciousness.
- *Amygdala*   A collection of cell nuclei lying just below the cerebral cortex, which are important for emotional responses.
- *Cerebral cortex*   Cortical neurons are responsible for all higher level sensory and cognitive functions, including perception, memory,

language, attention, and thought. Different areas of cortex specialize in different functions.

- *Cerebellum*   A large complex structure sitting at the back of brain, below the cerebral cortex and behind the brain stem. One of its functions is the unconscious control of movement, posture, and balance.

The fact that incoming sensory signals connect with all of these major structures in the brain demonstrates how critical the signals are for survival. A close examination of the various paths that the signals take through these structures can reveal exactly how the signals drive behavior.

Skin mechanoreceptors and nociceptors

The individual nerves carrying signals from receptors in the skin converge on the spinal cord. Both mechanoreceptors and **nociceptors** have cell bodies in the spinal cord, but after this their routes diverge. Each mechanoreceptor axon travels all the way up the spinal cord to terminate in the brain stem, where a second neuron relays the signal on to the thalamus. Some nerves are very long, because they travel all the way from a receptor ending in a body extremity to the brain stem. Nociceptor axons, on the other hand, terminate as soon as they enter the spinal cord; a second neuron relays the signal right up to the thalamus (see Figure 2.2). Why this difference between skin mechanoreceptors and nociceptors? Dangerous stimuli require a rapid withdrawal response. Nociceptor axons terminate in the spinal cord because this allows a branch line to carry signals straight back out to the muscles. Signals travel to the muscles to trigger a rapid reflexive withdrawal response to dangerous stimulation. This response to sensory input is literally a 'no-brainer' because it bypasses the brain completely. The signals that do reach the thalamus are passed on to the cortex to mediate perception of touch or pain.

Neural connections in the brain stem do not simply pass the incoming mechanoreceptor signals on to the thalamus, but fundamentally alter the character of the signal as illustrated in Figure 2.3. Three sensory neurons originating on the forearm (a, b, c) connect with neurons in the brain stem (A, B, C). Neurons A and C have branching connections to neuron B, and these

Key Term

Nociceptor. A class of sensory receptor that has no specialized nerve ending, but responds to dangerously intense stimuli associated with pain sensations.

connections are inhibitory so they act to attenuate any signals generated by B. The area of skin that influences neuron B's activity necessarily incorporates the areas covered by all three neurons a, b, and c. This area is known as the **receptive field** of neuron B. The particular way that the responses from a, b, and c combine determines the character of neuron B's response to stimulation. The response of neuron B increases when stimulation falls in one part of the forearm (the area labeled +), and decreases when stimulation falls in an adjacent area (the area labeled −). Recordings of activity in real cells have shown that many receptive fields on the skin are circular and concentrically organized in just the way illustrated in Figure 2.3. The center of the receptive field is excitatory, by virtue of signals traveling from neuron b, while the surround is inhibitory, by virtue of the lateral inhibition triggered by activity in neurons a and c. Thus, neuron B responds strongly to touch stimulation that is confined to a small area in the center of the receptive field, but weakly to stimulation that covers the whole receptive field. The benefits of this kind of receptive field organization will be discussed later on, when it is encountered again in the visual sense.

Key Term

Receptive field. The area of a receptive surface such as the skin or the retina in which stimulation causes a sensory neuron to respond.

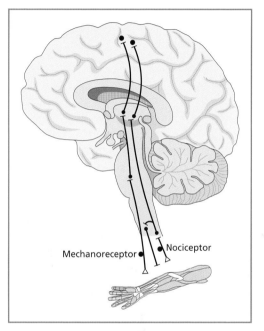

Figure 2.2 Ascending pathways for nociceptors and skin mechanoreceptors. Nociceptor axons terminate in the spinal cord, while mechanoreceptor axons travel up the spinal cord to terminate in the brain stem. Both pathways have a relay in the thalamus on the way to the cerebral cortex. A spinal reflex circuit in the nociceptor pathway provides rapid withdrawal responses to dangerous stimulation.

Cochlear and vestibular mechanoreceptors

Fibers in the cochlear and vestibular nerves terminate in the brain stem, in the cochlear and vestibular nucleus respectively. At least two additional synapses send the signals on to the thalamus (see Figure 2.4). Axons from the cochlear nucleus split into two paths. One path processes information about sound wave frequency, which you hear perceptually as pitch. Recall from the previous chapter that auditory nerve fibers contain pitch information by virtue

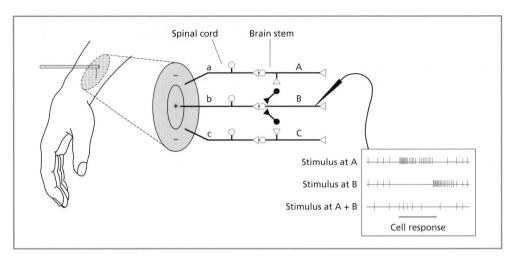

Figure 2.3 Receptive fields in the mechanoreceptor pathway. An electrode records neural impulses in brain stem neuron B resulting from tactile stimulation of the forearm. Activity increases when the area labeled '+' is stimulated (because of activity in neurons such as b), but decreases when the area labeled '−' is stimulated, because of inhibition spreading from neurons such as A and C.

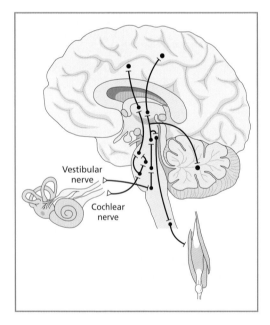

Figure 2.4 Pathways for cochlear and vestibular mechanoreceptors. Both involve a complex set of connections in the brain stem, before ascending to the thalamus and cerebral cortex. The vestibular pathway contains branches to the cerebellum and to the muscles controlling posture and eye movement.

of their location on the basilar membrane, and by the temporal pattern of their discharge. The other path combines signals from the two ears, so that cells in the brain stem can encode the direction in space from which sounds originate. Differences in the timing and intensity of sounds arriving at the two ears are used to encode sound source direction. Sounds toward the left arrive at the left ear slightly before the right ear, and may also be slightly louder (the head gets in the way of high-frequency sounds, but low-frequency sound waves can pass over and around the head). Inter-aural timing and intensity differences are detected by specialized cells in the brain stem. These two separate processing paths continue up to the cerebral cortex (Semple & Scott, 2003).

Axons from the vestibular nucleus also split into two paths. One continues up to the thalamus and the other branches off towards the cerebellum. Vestibular input to the cerebellum is used for regulating posture and balance. Reflex circuits in the brain stem also receive input from the vestibular nuclei, and send projections back down to the spinal cord as well as to the eye muscles. These circuits mediate reflexive control of body posture, head position, and gaze direction. Reflexive eye movements are called the **vestibulo-ocular reflexes**. When your head rotates in one direction, your eyes reflexively rotate in the opposite direction in order to maintain a stable visual image on your retina. Vestibular responses triggered by head movement are fed via the brain stem to muscles controlling your eyes, causing them to move in a way that exactly compensates for the head motion and so maintains a stable retinal image.

Cells in the thalamus carrying signals in the cochlear and vestibular pathways send projections to different areas of the cerebral cortex. The cortical projection in the vestibular pathway is relatively small, and may mediate perception of balance.

Chemoreceptors

The axons carrying gustatory signals terminate in the brain stem, and projections from there arrive at the thalamus (Figure 2.5). Signals from the thalamus then terminate in the primary gustatory cortex. Olfactory projections are quite different. The receptor fibers make synaptic contact with **mitral cells** in a projection of the brain called the **olfactory bulb**, which lies just above and behind the nose. Although the nose contains millions of individual receptors, there are only forty to fifty thousand

Key Terms

Vestibulo-ocular reflexes. Reflex circuits that include vestibular receptors and eye muscles, which control eye movements that compensate for head movements to maintain a stable retinal image.

Mitral cell. A neuron in the olfactory bulb that receives signals from olfactory receptor cells and relays them to the brain.

Olfactory bulb. A mass of neurons projecting from the brain behind the nose, which contains the mitral cells that carry olfactory responses.

DISCUSS AND DEBATE

To demonstrate the importance of the vestibulo-ocular reflex for maintaining visual stability, hold your head stationary and shake this book rapidly from to side. Notice that the print becomes so blurred that it is illegible. Now keep the book stationary but shake your head rapidly from side to side. Now the print remains perfectly readable. Your head bobs up and down while you walk; next time you take a walk, notice how your eyes rotate in their sockets in time with your head bobs, so you can see clearly where you are heading.

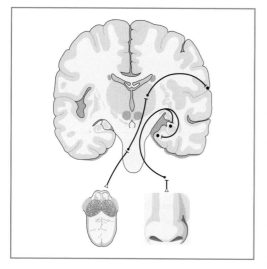

Figure 2.5 Pathways for chemoreceptors. Gustatory receptor axons terminate in the brain stem, with an ongoing projection to the thalamus and cortex. Olfactory signals do not pass through the thalamus on the way to the amygdala and cortex.

mitral cells in the olfactory bulb, so many receptor axons converge onto each mitral cell. This convergence is highly ordered; each mitral cell receives projections from only one of the hundreds of different receptor types in the nose. Figure 1.6 showed that a different subset of olfactory receptors is activated by each chemical compound you can identify. At the level of the olfactory bulb, only a subset of mitral cells is activated by each compound. So the ascending signals from the olfactory bulb contain information about the identity of olfactory stimuli. Given the several hundred different kinds of chemoreceptor and mitral cell in the human olfactory system, Malnic *et al.* (1999) estimated that we could in principle distinguish between millions of different odor compounds.

Uniquely among the sensory pathways, some olfactory signals do not have a synapse in the thalamus on their route to the cortex. So some olfactory signals arrive at the cortex without the moderating influence of the thalamus. Interestingly the olfactory sense uses the oldest parts of the brain, in terms of phylogenetics (evolutionary timing).

Photoreceptors

The path taken by photoreceptor signals involves four synapses (Figure 2.6). The first two are actually in the eye itself. For most optic nerve fibers the third synapse is the thalamus en route to the visual cortex, but a small number of optic nerve fibers branch off to terminate in the midbrain or brain stem. These branches are important for directing attention, regulating the 'body clock', and controlling pupil diameter.

Although there are over 120 million photoreceptors in each eye, only one million optic nerve fibers leave the eye. The first two synapses achieve a massive convergence of responses from many photoreceptors onto relatively few **retinal ganglion cells,**

Key Term

Retinal ganglion cell. A class of retinal cell whose fibers form the optic nerve, carrying the output signal from the retina.

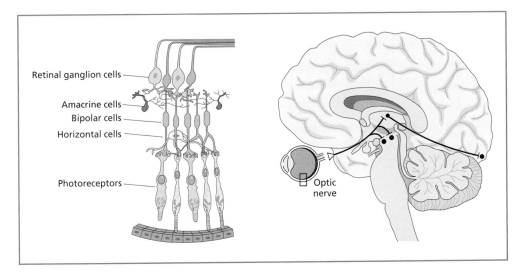

Retinal ganglion cells
Amacrine cells
Bipolar cells
Horizontal cells
Photoreceptors
Optic nerve

Figure 2.6 Pathways for photoreceptors. There are two synapses in the eye (left); signals then travel towards the brain along ganglion cell fibers (optic nerve). Most fibers terminate in the thalamus, though some branch off to terminate in the midbrain or brain stem. Thalamic cells project to primary visual cortex, located at the rear of the brain.

whose fibers form the optic nerve. The network of connections in the retina ensures that essential information is preserved during the convergence from photoreceptors to ganglion cells (Figure 2.6, left).

Bipolar cells connect vertically through the retina towards ganglion cells, while **horizontal cells** and **amacrine cells** connect horizontally across the retina. Each ganglion cell has a receptive field defined by the area of retina covered by the photoreceptors that connect to it. As mentioned earlier, on average 120 receptors must connect to each ganglion cell to achieve the necessary degree of convergence in the optic nerve output. The eye manages this convergence in a very clever way that preserves as much information as possible. In the center of the retina (the fovea, described in Chapter 1), which receives an image of the point on which you are fixating at any given moment, each ganglion cell is connected to only about seven photoreceptors (mostly cones). In the periphery

Key Terms

Bipolar cell. A class of retinal cell that conveys responses from the photoreceptors to retinal ganglion cells. Different subtypes carry responses from rods and from cones.

Horizontal cell. A class of retinal cell whose axons spread laterally, making contact with several photoreceptors.

Amacrine cell. A class of retinal cell whose axons spread laterally in deeper retinal layers, making contact with many bipolar and ganglion cells.

DISCUSS AND DEBATE

To demonstrate how the different retinal distributions of rod and cone photoreceptors affect vision, notice that: (1) in bright conditions (while you are reading this book), you can see best where you are looking at any given moment, so only the most central three or so words are legible; (2) outdoors at night you can see dim lights and stars only when they are just away from where you are looking.

---

of the retina each ganglion cell connects to many tens of photoreceptors (mostly rods). Consequently ganglion cells in central vision carry very precise information about the image because their receptive field covers a very small area of retina. Ganglion cells out in the periphery, on the other hand, have very large receptive fields, so they discard spatial detail but their large catchment area gives them high sensitivity to very dim light (and they are fed by rods that are more plentiful in the periphery). Variation in ganglion cell receptive field size explains why your ability to see detail is quite poor at low light levels.

As in the case of touch illustrated in Figure 2.3, ganglion cell receptive fields are circular and concentric. In some ganglion cells the center of the receptive field is excitatory and the surround is inhibitory (Figure 2.7, top). Other ganglion cells have the opposite arrangement (Figure 2.7, bottom). Furthermore cells in the center of the retina are fed only by cones, and this gives them sensitivity to color (wavelength, strictly speaking). Some ganglion cells have a red cone in the center and mostly green cones in the surround, and other cells have the opposite arrangement. The larger receptive fields out in the periphery have a mixture of cone types in both center and surround, so do not show sensitivity to color (see Lennie, 2000).

Thus, ganglion cells select only certain aspects of the image for transmission to the brain. Some cells signal variations in illumination only, while others signal variations in wavelength as well. In all cases constant illumination provokes only a weak response. So by the time signals leave the eye the visual system has already begun the process of analyzing the information contained in the image. Only useful information about variation in illumination and wavelength is preserved; unchanging illumination is largely ignored.

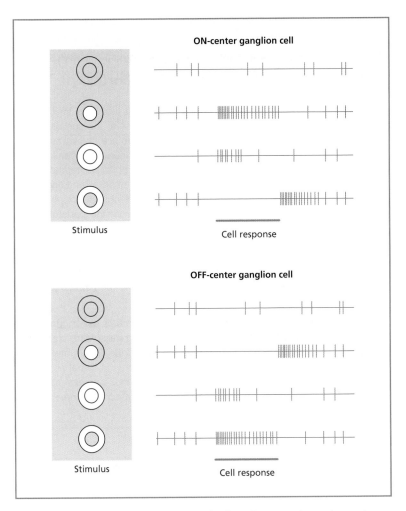

Figure 2.7 Ganglion cell receptive fields. Light stimuli are shown superimposed on center–surround receptive fields (left). Neural impulses are shown by vertical marks on the horizontal time axis (right). The thick bars show the duration of the stimuli. On-center cells are turned on by light in the center, while off-center cells are turned off. The opposite response occurs in the surround. There is little response when the entire receptive field is illuminated.

Cells in the thalamus that receive input from the optic nerve send projections to an area of cortex known as visual cortex. Thalamic cells have the same general receptive field layout as the ganglion cells that project to them, namely a circularly symmetrical, antagonistic center–surround organization.

KEY CONCEPT

Anatomy of the cerebral cortex

The surface area of the cerebral cortex is so great that it fits inside the skull only because it is highly convoluted. The ridges of the convolutions are known as gyri (singular, gyrus), and the valleys are known as sulci (singular, sulcus), or fissures if they are especially deep. Conventionally the surface of the cortex is divided into four zones or lobes, named after the bones that lie above them: the frontal, parietal, temporal, and occipital lobes (see Figure 2.8). The frontal lobe lies at the front (anterior), behind the frontal bone of the forehead and separated from the parietal lobe by the central sulcus. The temporal lobe lies behind the temple at the side of the head, separated from the frontal lobe by the lateral fissure. The parietal lobe lies rearward of the central sulcus, and above the lateral fissure. The occipital lobe occupies the back (posterior) surface of the cortex. The boundary between the occipital lobe and the parietal lobe is rather arbitrary.

Research has shown that each lobe performs a specific set of cognitive functions. The frontal lobe is essential for controlling and planning behavior (and is the most recently developed of the four lobes); the temporal lobe processes sounds and also specializes in visual recognition; the parietal lobe processes body sensations and is also essential for guiding selective attention to stimuli; and the occipital cortex is devoted to visual processing.

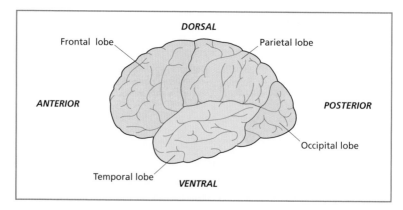

Figure 2.8 The four lobes of each cerebral hemisphere, and some important directional terms (in italics).

Cortical processing

The seven distinct pathways from the sensory receptors arrive in six different cortical areas, which are known as cortical receiving areas, or primary sensory areas. Figure 2.9 illustrates the locations of these six areas. Primary visual cortex is in the occipital lobe, and runs deep into the calcarine fissure. Primary auditory cortex lies in the temporal lobe, mostly in the lateral fissure. Note that, although skin mechanoreceptors and nociceptors follow different paths (Figure 2.2), they arrive in the same area of cortex, so in cortical terms at least they can be considered as a single sense, often called 'somatosensation' or body sense. Primary somatosensory cortex is a strip of parietal cortex running vertically from the top of the head down each side. The cortical receiving areas for chemoreceptors and vestibular mechanoreceptors occupy relatively small areas of primary cortex in the parietal and temporal lobes, as well as in the orbitofrontal cortex of the frontal lobe (Martin, 2004).

Each cortical receiving area is only the first stage of processing for most senses. Secondary cortical areas lie adjacent to the primary areas, and receive inputs from them. In vision, for example, there are

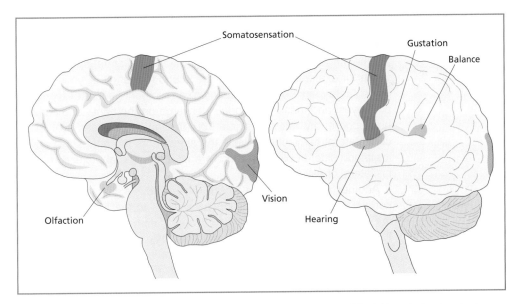

Figure 2.9 Cortical receiving areas for the six sensory systems. Left: Medial view of the right cerebral cortex, showing areas lying in the longitudinal fissure that divides the two hemispheres. Right: Lateral view of the left hemisphere, showing areas visible on the lateral surface of the cortex.

at least five secondary areas, and a number of additional areas that receive projections from these secondary areas. In hearing, a belt of secondary cortex surrounds primary auditory cortex. Olfaction and gustation appear to converge on a common area of secondary cortex, which may play a role in flavor perception (Rolls, 2006). The total cortical area devoted to different senses varies dramatically. Vision consumes by far the largest area of cortical real estate, while balance has hardly any cortical representation. These differences partly reflect the processing demands in each sensory system. Recall from the previous chapter that photoreceptors are far more numerous than any other receptor type and this reflects the complexity of visual stimuli, which are extended in two spatial dimensions as well as in time. Variations in cortical area also reflect the relative importance of different senses to humans. The picture is different in other species. Bats, for instance, have a much greater cortical representation for hearing, while rats have a large somatosensory representation of their whiskers (Krubitzer, 1995).

The brain is divided into two seemingly symmetrical halves or hemispheres, left and right, which are connected together by the largest band of fibers in the brain, known as the corpus callosum. In general, sensory signals originating in receptors on one side of the body cross over to arrive in the cerebral hemisphere on the other (contralateral) side of the body, rather than staying on the same (ipsilateral) side of the body. However there are exceptions to this rule. In vision and hearing there are both contralateral and ipsilateral projections. In vision for example, each part of the scene to the left of your point of binocular (two-eyed) fixation at any given moment generates signals in both eyes, and these two signals converge on the right-hand cerebral hemisphere; the relevant signal from the left eye crosses over to the contralateral hemisphere, while the signal from the right stays on the ipsilateral side. In olfaction there are no contralateral projections, only ipsilateral ones.

Another general feature of all the senses is that each sensory cortical area sends a projection back down to the thalamus. Indeed the majority of axons that arrive in the thalamus are not ascending fibers from the sensory periphery, but descending fibers from the cortex. In the case of vision, for example, retinal input accounts for only 10% of the synapses onto neurons in the lateral geniculate nucleus of the thalamus; 30% of the input comes from the visual cortex (Sillito & Jones, 2002). So the cortex has an opportunity to directly influence thalamic activity and so shape its own input. This feedback from the cortex is thought to serve two functions. First it sharpens up the stimulus tuning of thalamic cells, making them respond more selectively to stimulus inputs. Second, it modulates the relative strength of different incoming signals, boosting some relative to others. This feedback may allow the cortex to focus processing on some sensory inputs at the expense of others, and so direct attention only to certain stimuli.

Signals originating from nociceptors are also fed back down from the cortex to the brain stem, permitting central modulation of pain signals. So ascending pain signals from the extremities can be modulated by descending signals from the brain. This downward information flow may be responsible for 'mind over matter' effects such as the analgesic effects of dummy placebo pills, and the absence of pain felt by soldiers sustaining horrific injuries in the height of battle.

Parallel pathways

There is a good deal of evidence that sensory processing divides into two parallel but interconnected pathways or 'streams' through the brain, one passing through dorsal areas of the cortex (back and upper part of the brain) from the occipital lobe to the parietal lobe, and the other passing through ventral areas of the cortex (front and lower part of the brain) from the occipital lobe to the temporal lobe. However there is still uncertainty and disagreement regarding the best way to characterize the difference between the two streams. One scheme divides them into the dorsal 'where' and ventral 'what' pathways (Ungerleider & Mishkin, 1982): the 'what' pathway is concerned with the identification of objects, and the 'where' pathway is concerned with their location. An alternative scheme divides the two pathways into the dorsal 'action' and ventral 'perception' pathways (Goodale & Milner, 1992): The 'perception' pathway is concerned with conscious awareness of the environment, and the function of the 'action' pathway is to engage with the environment, rather than to represent it. Whichever characterization of the two pathways is ultimately the more useful, evidence indicates that the distinction between them is not clear-cut. There are extensive connections between the two streams, and a good deal of overlap in terms of functional properties.

Evaluation

By the time sensory signals reach the cortex, they have sorted themselves out anatomically into six distinct systems, with correspondingly distinct perceptual modalities: Vision, hearing, touch/pain, balance, smell, and taste. All of the sensory pathways involve both subcortical and cortical processing centers, which reflect the multitude of ways in which sensory information is used by the brain. Subcortical neural networks, mostly in the brain stem, mediate fast, unconscious responses to sensory input, such as orienting to visual or auditory stimuli, or withdrawal from dangerous stimuli. They also achieve some degree of sensory integration, particularly in terms of vestibular control of balance and visual stability. Cortical processes mediate more sophisticated, conscious responses to sensory input, particularly evaluation and recognition of current stimuli. Thalamic feedback gives the brain control over what and how stimuli reach conscious levels of processing.

RESEARCH QUESTION

Why can't you tickle yourself?

No matter how ticklish you are, you cannot tickle yourself – an obvious but rather mysterious aspect of somatosensation. To investigate why this might be so, Blakemore *et al.* (2000) created a robotic tickling machine. When the experimental participant pressed a button, a robotic arm brushed a piece of foam across the participant's hand. As one might expect, this did not produce a tickle sensation. When there was a delay of about one fifth of a second between the button press and the arm movement, the sensation of tickle increased. Clearly the brain's response to the stimuli (tickle versus no tickle) depends on timing. Other experiments identified the cerebellum (described earlier in the chapter and pictured in Figure 2.1) as the likely source of the signals that modulated the sensation of tickle. Why?

The explanation runs as follows. You need to know the causes of things if you are to understand what is happening in the world. So it is vital for the brain to be able to distinguish between events triggered by your own actions and events triggered by other agents. The tickle experiments indicate that the brain has specialized neural circuits that predict the sensory consequences of your own actions. If the prediction matches the actual sensory stimulation, then the sensory stimulation can be discounted to a certain extent. The brain region that does this job is the cerebellum. It receives a copy of all movement commands, as well as information from all the senses. If a self-generated action immediately precedes a sensation, such as when you tickle yourself, then the cerebellum infers that one caused the other and attenuates the response to the sensation. If action and sensation do not occur close together, the causal link between them is broken and a stronger, tickling sensation is felt.

Summary

- Signals from the four classes of sensory receptor (mecha-noreceptors, chemoreceptors, photoreceptors, nociceptors) are carried to the cerebral cortex along a series of dedicated neural pathways.
- The signals pass through a series of connection points en route, allowing them to branch into other brain regions. All signals except those from olfactory receptors pass through the thalamus on the way to the cortex.
- The nociceptor pathway includes a reflex circuit in the spinal cord, which generates automatic muscle responses to dangerous stimulation. Body mechanoreceptor and noci-ceptor signals share the same cortical destination, the primary somatosensory cortex.
- Cochlear and vestibular pathways involve a complex set of serial and parallel routes. Separate auditory pathways specialize in extracting sound frequency and direction. The vestibular pathway includes a reflex circuit to maintain gaze stability during head movements.
- Olfactory and gustatory receptor signals arrive in different cortical regions, but merge together in a secondary area of cortex.
- Photoreceptor responses undergo significant modification before they leave the retina, so that responses emphasize changes in retinal illumination. Retinal ganglion receptive fields have a center–surround organization.
- Sensory signals destined for the cortex arrive in one of six distinct primary cortical areas. Signals from primary cortex are sent to secondary cortical areas, as well as back down to the thalamus, and to other structures such as the cere-bellum.

REFLECTIVE EXERCISE

1. A receptive field is:
   a. The first destination of incoming fibers in the cortex
   b. The area of vision you can see with both eyes
   c. The stimulus area that causes a cell to respond
   d. Only found on the forearm

2. Different sensory pathways contain different numbers of synapses (e.g. four for vision, two for olfaction). Discuss the implications of these differences for perception.

3. Evaluate the safety implications of vestibular reflexes for driving or flying.

FURTHER READING

- Braz, J.M., Nassar, M.A., Wood, J.N., & Basbaum, A.I. (2005) Parallel 'pain' pathways arise from subpopulations of primary afferent nociceptor. *Neuron, 47*, 787–793.
- Farivar, R. (2009) Dorsal–ventral integration in object recognition. *Brain Research Reviews, 61*, 144–153.
- Firestein, S. (2001) How the olfactory system makes sense of scents. *Nature, 413*, 211–218.
- Hubel, D.H., & Wiesel, T.N. (1977) Functional architecture of macaque monkey visual cortex. *Proceedings of the Royal Society of London, Series B, 198*, 1–59.
- Lennie, P. (2000) Color vision: putting it all together. *Current Biology, 10*, R589–R591.
- Rolls, E.T. (2006) Brain mechanisms underlying flavour and appetite. *Philosophical Transactions of the Royal Society, B, 361*, 1123–1136.

The senses and the brain

3

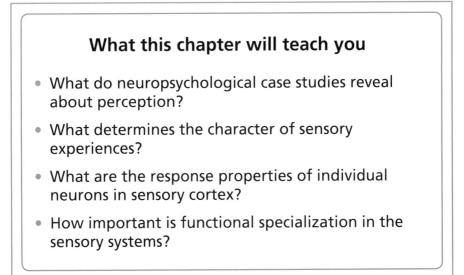

What this chapter will teach you

- What do neuropsychological case studies reveal about perception?
- What determines the character of sensory experiences?
- What are the response properties of individual neurons in sensory cortex?
- How important is functional specialization in the sensory systems?

Introduction

You saw in Chapter 2 that the anatomy of the sensory pathways divides the senses into six modalities, each with its own cortical receiving area. Anatomy studies the structure of each sensory system – the number of synapses, the paths taken by the nerves, their destination in the cortex. However it cannot reveal the functional properties of the sensory systems, which have to do with their *physiology*. How do the various components of the sensory systems work? What roles do they play in perception? Physiological function was touched on in Chapter 2, when discussing the properties of receptive fields in somatosensation and vision. This chapter considers the physiology of the sensory systems in more detail.

A key feature of sensory physiology is specialization. Sensory receptor cells are very diverse anatomically because they specialize in transducing particular forms of external energy (light, sound, pressure) into neural signals. On the other hand, nerve cells in the sensory pathways and cortex all have the same components (though their detailed anatomy may vary), which were described in Chapter 1: a cell body, dendrites that receive inputs from other neurons, and an axon to carry the cell's activity to other cells. All nerve cells also generate the same kind of electrical signals in the form of action potentials – waves of electrical activity that travel along the axon to the nerve ending. If one inspected an individual nerve cell in a microscope, or monitored its electrical activity using a fine recording electrode, that information alone would give no clue about the *function* it performed in the nervous system. Yet sensory cells and their signals do perform highly specialized functions, and in order to understand the sensory systems it is important to work out what these functions are. A range of different research techniques have been developed for studying perceptual function. The first technique to be used systematically involves observing how brain damage affects perception.

Clinical case studies

Much has been learned about specialization of function from the experiences of individuals who have suffered damage to part of their sensory system. If some particular perceptual dysfunction always occurs when a particular neural structure is damaged, then one can draw inferences about the function of the relevant structure. Not surprisingly, damage to sensory receptors causes fundamental impairment. For instance, infection or exposure to a dangerously loud sound such as an explosion can permanently damage cochlear hair cells and so cause long-term hearing loss, known as sensorineural hearing loss. Sounds appear distorted and indistinct, and hearing aids are of limited use because they simply

Key Terms

Transduction. The process by which sensory receptor cells convert environmental energy into electrical signals.

Sensorineural hearing loss. Permanent deafness caused by damage to cochlear hair cells.

amplify the incoming sound. Dysfunction and damage in hair cells of the vestibular organ have markedly different consequences: dizziness, nausea, and uncontrollable eye movements. If the problem is confined to only one of the semi-circular canals, the symptoms may be experienced only when the head is held at a particular angle, reflecting the function of that particular canal (Parnes *et al.*, 2003).

In rare cases a viral illness can cause the body's defences to attack its own cells. For one individual known as IW, the attack destroyed the afferent axons of mechanoreceptor cells in his skin and muscles (Cole, 1998). As a result IW lost his ability to sense touch and body position. He is still capable of movement, and can sense heat, pain, and muscle fatigue because nociceptor axons were spared, but he no longer has precise control of his posture or movement. Even everyday actions such as sitting or walking are impossible without continuous, conscious visual monitoring of his body to keep track of body position and attitude. His arms, for instance, are likely to wave about aimlessly unless he can attend to them visually.

Damage in the cortex can cause a range of highly specific perceptual problems, reflecting its high degree of functional specialization. In a condition called asomatognosia, damage to an area of the right-hand cortex near the junction of the temporal and parietal lobes causes the patient to misidentify their left arm, and if damage includes the frontal lobe the patient may disown the arm entirely, often arguing that it is not their arm but 'the doctor's arm' (Feinberg *et al.*, 2010). In the case of vision the earliest discoveries of cortically induced blindness were made by a Japanese surgeon called Tatsuji Inouye, who studied soldiers injured during the Russo-Japanese war (1904–1905). The high-velocity rifles used in that conflict produced relatively clean, circumscribed brain injuries. So Inouye was able to trace the path of each bullet through the brain and found a precise, systematic relation between the area of damage in primary visual cortex and a circumscribed area of blindness known as a scotoma (Glickstein & Whitteridge, 1987). In this way he was able to show that the visual field is mapped in a highly ordered way across the surface of the primary visual cortex (an idea that you will explore in more detail later).

Damage in secondary visual cortex does not cause complete blindness, but instead makes an individual blind to a very specific aspect of the visual world. For example,

Key Terms

Asomatognosia. A clinical disorder in which the patient fails to recognize their own limbs on one side of the body, following damage in the right-hand cerebral cortex.

Scotoma. A small area of blindness in the field of view, caused by damage to the visual pathway or cortex.

damage to an area of secondary visual cortex known as V4 results in a clinical condition called **achromatopsia**, in which the patient can no longer see colors. The loss may be accompanied by other visual defects, depending on the area of damage (Zeki, 1990). Damage in another secondary visual area known as MT causes **akinetopsia**, an inability to see movement. Zihl *et al.* (1983) reported a case in which the patient had difficulties in any task that required judgment of image motion. It was difficult to pour tea into a cup without spilling it because she could not perceive the liquid rising in the cup. She could not cross a road safely because vehicles seemed to appear in different places unpredictably. Damage to other areas of secondary cortex causes even more perplexing conditions, grouped together under the term **agnosia**, in which the affected individuals have no difficulty in seeing but cannot make sense of what they see (Farah, 2004). They cannot recognize objects on sight, despite being able to name them by other means (touch or sound), and to draw them by simple copying. In some cases the condition appears to be limited to recognition of faces (**prosopagnosia**). These cases indicate that different areas of secondary visual cortex specialize in processing very specific perceptual attributes.

Brain stimulation studies

The neurosurgeon Wilder Penfield published detailed accounts of the brain operations he performed in the 1950s to treat epilepsy. Penfield's technique was to destroy the brain cells whose activity triggered epileptic seizures, but in order to minimize side-effects he needed to identify the functions performed by particular areas of cortical tissue. So the patient was anesthetized but awake during the surgery, and Penfield mapped out the function of exposed areas of cortex by applying small electrical currents directly to the cortical tissue. Patients reported feeling sensations that depended on the area stimulated. Figure 3.1 shows a drawing of a specific case, with the exposed area of cortex and numbered locations identifying stimulation sites. Here is Penfield's record of the sensations reported following stimulation (Penfield, 1958, p. 28):

Key Terms

Achromatopsia. A clinical disorder in which the patient is unable to perceive color, usually because of damage to an area of secondary visual cortex called V4.

Akinetopsia. A rare neurological disorder also known as 'motion blindness', in which the patient cannot perceive visual movement despite being able to recognize and locate objects visually; usually caused by damage to an area of secondary visual cortex called MT.

Agnosia. A clinical disorder in which the patient is unable to visually perceive shapes or objects.

Prosopagnosia. A clinical disorder in which the patient is unable to recognize faces.

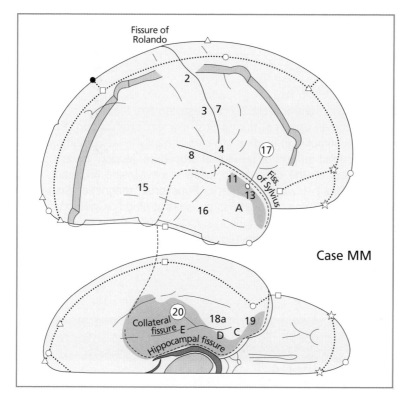

Figure 3.1 Area of cortical tissue exposed during neurosurgery performed by Wilder Penfield, labeled with the sites of stimulation. From Penfield (1958). Reproduced with permission from Liverpool University Press.

Stimulation at point 2 – sensation in thumb and index finger. She called it 'quivering', 'tingling'.

3 – 'Same feeling on the left side of my tongue'.

7 – Movement of the tongue.

4 – 'Yes, a feeling at the back of my throat like nausea.'

8 – She said 'No'. Then she said, 'Yes, I suddenly cannot hear'. This is, obviously, the border of auditory sensory cortex.

Other patients stimulated in presumed visual cortex reported seeing colored, flickering, or moving lights. Penfield's records offer dramatic, direct evidence of the link between specific cortical areas and particular sensations. They produced remarkably precise maps of cortical function, as you will see later. A more recent and engaging account of this kind of work can be found in Calvin and Ojemann (1994).

Neuroimaging

In traditional neuropsychological case studies the area of damage only becomes apparent during post-mortem examination. Penfield's electrical stimulation studies are clearly highly invasive and can only be performed as part of a medical procedure. Modern neuroimaging techniques, on the other hand, allow a view inside an intact, living brain without invasive surgery. Functional magnetic resonance imaging (fMRI, see box) detects changes in blood oxygen concentration as a marker for changes in neural activity in the brain. It builds up a picture of the brain regions activated by particular sensory stimuli.

KEY CONCEPT

Functional magnetic resonance imaging (fMRI)

Structural imaging techniques were originally developed in the 1970s for use in medical diagnosis. One technique, known as magnetic resonance imaging (MRI), exploits the magnetic properties of hydrogen nuclei. The body is scanned with an intense magnetic field to build up an image of the distribution of hydrogen nuclei. Cells, axons, fluid, tissue, and bones all differ in the concentration of hydrogen nuclei, so it is possible to build up a detailed picture of the structural composition of the body, including the brain. Brain abnormalities or damage can be identified non-invasively from MRI scans.

MRI scans can reveal a lot about structure, but only a little about function (when combined with clinical assessments). In the late 1980s a variant of MRI technology, called functional magnetic resonance imaging (fMRI), was developed. It can reveal much more about function. It is based on the fact that mental activity is correlated with neural activity, and neural activity in turn requires oxygen. So changes in mental activity cause changes in blood oxygenation within the brain. The concentration of oxygen in the blood affects the magnetic properties of hemoglobin, an effect called the *blood oxygen level dependent* (BOLD) response. An fMRI scanner detects regional variations in BOLD response caused by variations in mental activity, so it is possible to build a detailed picture of the brain areas activated during specific mental activities. In a typical fMRI experiment the participant is placed in the scanner and engages in two tasks in alternation. In the simplest case this may involve alternately inspecting two different visual patterns, such as a moving pattern and a stationary one. Brain areas that respond only to the moving pattern will show an alternation in BOLD response that mirrors the alternation in the stimulus. It is therefore possible to identify the brain areas specifically associated with processing motion information (see main text).

As an example, consider the results of an fMRI study of motion perception that compared responses to moving and static stimuli in primary visual cortex (V1), and in secondary visual area MT (Tootell *et al.*, 1995).

The solid line in Figure 3.2 shows the change in signal in V1 as the stimulus alternated between moving and static presentations. Primary visual cortex responds equally well to both. The dashed line in Figure 3.2 shows the signal change in MT during stimulus alternation. MT responds only to the moving stimuli, which can be taken as evidence that this area has a speciality for processing motion. This same area was identified as the focus of damage in the patient described earlier, who suffered from akinetopsia.

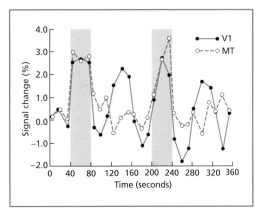

Figure 3.2 Results of an fMRI experiment in which the visual stimulus alternated between moving (shaded) and static patterns. Primary visual cortex responded equally to the two patterns (solid line), whereas extrastriate area MT responded only to the moving stimulus (dashed line). Adapted from Tootell *et al.* (1995).

Neuroimaging studies usefully confirm and extend the picture of cortical organization summarized in Figure 2.8: Each sensory pathway projects to a dedicated cortical receiving area; in most senses adjacent areas of secondary cortex perform a more detailed analysis of the sensory information. Nevertheless fMRI research has its limitations. Changes in blood oxygenation have a relatively slow time course, at least in the time-scale of neural impulses, so fMRI cannot say much about variations in neural processing over very short time periods. Furthermore the spatial resolution of fMRI is currently around 1 millimeter, an area that contains hundreds of thousands of cells (Hubel & Wiesel, 1977), so it cannot reveal anything about function at the microscopic level at which individual cells operate.

Single-unit recordings

The most direct way to study the function of individual nerve cells is to record their electrical response to sensory stimulation, but the technical challenge is formidable because neurons are extremely small. A typical cell body is only one fiftieth of a millimeter in diameter, while nerve fiber diameters are ten times smaller. Nevertheless the technique was first perfected in the 1920s by Edgar Adrian, a physiologist working at Cambridge University in the UK. He succeeded in recording nerve impulses from single sensory nerves in a frog's muscle (Adrian & Zotterman, 1926; see Figure 5.4, p. 82). Some of the earliest recordings of single-unit responses to visual stimulation were made in the 1950s by Stephen Kuffler at Johns Hopkins University in the USA (Kuffler, 1953). He inserted fine recording electrodes into the eye of an awake, anesthetized cat, and was able to record activity from individual retinal ganglion cells in response to small spots of light projected onto the animal's retina. He found that each ganglion cell responded only when light fell within a circumscribed area of the retina, which defined the cell's receptive field. The receptive field was divided into two concentric regions. Light in one region increased the cell's activity, while light in the other region decreased its activity. Just such a receptive field was illustrated in Figure 1.7, and Kuffler was one of the first researchers to describe it. Similar recordings were also reported at about the same time by Horace Barlow at Cambridge University, working in the frog's retina (Barlow, 1953).

Two young post-doctoral researchers working in Stephen Kuffler's laboratory took up his technique of projecting small, precisely defined stimuli onto the cat's retina, and recording responses in single neurons. However David Hubel and Torsten Wiesel recorded from cells in the animal's primary visual cortex, rather than in its retina. They found, almost by accident, that the great majority of cortical cells were much more selective than those in the retina. Initially Hubel and Wiesel found cells that responded only when a line moved through the receptive field in a particular direction. Different cells responded best to different directions. They also found cells that were not direction selective, but did respond selectively to line or edge orientation (Hubel & Wiesel, 1959). Hubel and Wiesel won the Nobel Prize in Physiology or Medicine in 1981 for the work they had begun in the late 1950s. Two examples of the kind of receptive field they observed are shown in Figure 3.3.

The cell at the top (a so-called 'simple' cortical cell) responds most strongly when a bar at the optimal orientation falls across the middle of the receptive field, rather than to one side or the other. The cell at the bottom (a so-called 'complex' cortical cell) responds to its preferred stimulus regardless of the bar's precise position in its receptive field. Other cells show preferences for other stimulus attributes; many respond well only when the bar moves in a particular direction; some respond to binocular input (depth) or to color.

So individual sensory cells in the visual cortex are highly specialized, responding only to a narrow range of stimuli. A similar high degree of specialization is shown in the other senses. In the auditory system individual cells respond to a very narrow range of sound frequencies (Palmer, 1995), or to sounds emanating from a particular direction in space (Fitzpatrick *et al.*, 1997). In somatosensory cortex individual cells respond only to touch in a specific body region. Moreover, each receives input from only one of the many types of mechanoreceptor cell (Mountcastle, 1957).

Even more remarkably, cortical cells are arranged very precisely in the cortex according to their stimulus preference. Cells with similar stimulus preferences are usually found very close to each other. In somatosensory cortex neighboring cells have receptive fields that are near to each other on the body. There is a steady progression in receptive field location as one advances across somatosensory cortex, so that the whole body is mapped on the cortex. Figure 3.4a shows a cross-section through half of the cortex, along a line running from the top of the head down the side to the ear (the blue area in Figure 2.9). One half of the body surface is represented along this

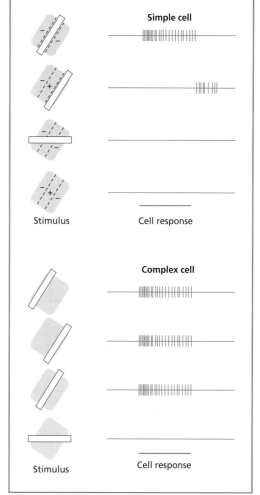

Stimulus

Simple cell

Cell response

Complex cell

Stimulus

Cell response

Figure 3.3 Stimulus selective responses of cells in the primary visual cortex. Some cells respond only when an oriented feature falls across the center of the elongated receptive field (top); other cells respond to optimally oriented features positioned anywhere in the receptive field (bottom).

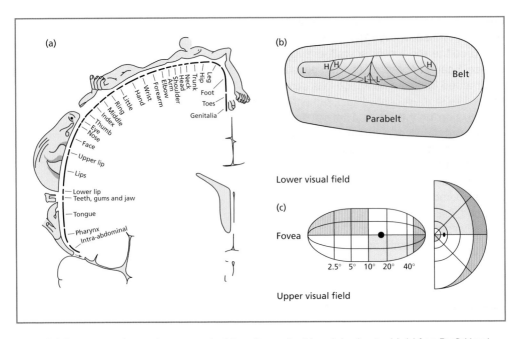

Figure 3.4 Sensory maps in somatosensory cortex (a), auditory cortex (b), and visual cortex (c). (a) from Penfield and Rasmussen (1950). (c) 1950 Gale, a part of Cengage Learning, Inc. Reproduced by permission. www.cengage.com/permissions

strip of cortex. Neurons near the top have a receptive field on the leg, while neurons near the ear have a receptive field inside the mouth (this map was first discovered by Penfield during his stimulation studies).

Figure 3.4b shows the surface of auditory cortex (an enlarged view of the grey area in Figure 2.9). Primary auditory cortex is in the center, surrounded by secondary areas (Kaas & Hackett, 2000). Cells with similar preferences for sound frequency lie close to each other in auditory cortex, and the cortical surface can be divided into a series of bands containing cells with the same preferred frequency (L means low-frequency preference; H means high-frequency preference).

The semi-circle on the right of Figure 3.4c represents the right-hand side of the **visual field**, assuming that fixation is at the center of the circle. The large moon-shaped crescent represents the far periphery, right in the 'corner' of the eye, and the small black dot is your blind spot. This half of the visual field is mapped out on the surface of the left-hand primary visual cortex (the red

Key Term

Visual field. The entire area of space that can be seen from the eye without changing its position.

area on Figure 2.9), shown by the oval shape to the left of Figure 3.4c. Visual cortical cells with receptive fields that are nearby in the visual field (and therefore nearby on the retina) lie near to each other in the cortex. Shaded areas on the cortical surface depicted in Figure 3.4c correspond to the same shaded areas in the visual field map (Tootell *et al.*, 1982).

These **sensory maps** often reveal gross inequalities in cortical processing resources. In the case of somatosensation (Figure 3.4a), some body regions such as the hands and face occupy a much greater cortical area than other regions such as the back and the legs. In vision, the central area of the retina (**fovea**; see Figure 1.7) occupies far more of the cortical surface than the peripheral part of the retina; about half of the cortical surface is devoted to an area of vision about as wide as your hand, if you hold it at arm's length and fixate at the center of it (compare the size of the corresponding shaded areas in Figure 3.4c). This variation in cortical processing is called **cortical magnification**. It shows that the area of cortex devoted to a given area of a receptive surface (such as the body or the retina) depends on the number of receptors in that part of the surface, not on the area of the surface itself. The fovea, for example, occupies a tiny area of the retina, but a very large area of the cortex; it contains the highest concentration of cone photoreceptors. Cortical magnification has profound consequences for perception as you shall see in the next chapter.

Evaluation

Physiological studies indicate that the cerebral cortex plays a dominant role in sensory experience. Cortical dominance explains the otherwise curious sensations reported by patients experiencing phantom limbs. Following amputation of a limb, most people report sensations that appear to be located on the missing 'phantom' limb. Unfortunately the majority of these sensations are painful ones. One striking feature of phantom limb experience was reported by Ramachandran and Hirstein (1998). When a patient with an amputated arm is stroked on the face, they may experience a touch sensation on their missing arm. Ramachandran and Hirstein (1998) reported the experiences of one

Key Terms

Sensory map. An ordered, topographical arrangement of sensory neurons that reflects the structure of the relevant sensory surface (the body, the retina, the cochlea).

Fovea. A small area at the center of the retina, containing many densely packed cone photoreceptors but no rods.

Cortical magnification. Distortion of a sensory cortical map that reflects the number of receptors devoted to each part of the sensory surface.

patient, VQ, whose arm was amputated following a road accident. When a point on his face was touched with a cotton swab, he felt a sensation on his arm or hand:

> Furthermore, the distribution of these points was not random . . . and there was a systematic one-to-one mapping between specific regions on the face and individual digits (e.g. from the cheek to the thumb, from the upper lip to the index finger and from the chin to the little finger). Typically the patient reports that he simultaneously felt the cotton swap touching his face and a tingling sensation in an individual digit.
>
> (p. 1609)

Similar experiences were reported by other patients. Recall from Figure 3.4 that the area of somatosensory cortex devoted to the face lies adjacent to the area devoted to the arm and hand. Ramachandran and Hirstein (1998) argue that, following amputation of the arm, afferent signals from the face invade the neighboring area of cortex formerly devoted to the arm. However, such is the nature of cortical dominance that signals arriving in the 'arm area' provoked by stimulation of the face are still experienced as being localized on the arm.

Phantom limb experiences indicate that what matters is not the origin of the signal, but its destination. Some recent work shows that this rule can sometimes be overridden. In one experiment, new-born ferrets had part of their sensory pathways surgically 're-wired' to direct visual input to the auditory cortex (von Melchner et al., 2000). Once reared to adulthood and trained to discriminate between visual and auditory stimuli, the 're-wired' animals appeared to treat visual stimulation arriving at auditory cortex as visual rather than auditory. What mattered was the source of the signals not the destination, in contradiction to the cortical dominance rule. von Melchner et al. (2000) concluded that during development sensory afferents can apparently instruct the cortex as to its sensory function. How? The 're-wired' animals did retain substantial normal wiring in the visual system, as well as the cross-modal connections mentioned above, and these may have played a role in training the auditory cortex to become visual. So it seems that cortical dominance can be overcome by deprivation or by re-wiring very early in perceptual development. However these examples seem to be exceptions that prove the rule. Recent work in this area on humans is described in the *Research Question* box.

RESEARCH QUESTION

Can a blind person 'see' with their visual cortex?

Recent research on humans has challenged the established view of cortical dominance in sensation, and has raised the intriguing possibility that in certain circumstances sensory experiences can be governed by the source of the signals, rather than by their cortical destination. In humans deprived of a particular sensory modality from birth, the deprived cortex can be invaded by other sensory modalities, in a similar way to that reported by Ramachandran and Hirstein (1998) for amputees. The auditory cortex of a deaf person may be activated by visual sign language; Braille reading by a trained blind subject may activate their visual cortex. What is the subjective character of activation in congenitally deprived cortex? To investigate this question, Kupers *et al.* (2006) trained congenitally blind subjects to recognize visual patterns using a 'tongue display unit' (TDU), which converts visual images into tactile stimulation. The TDU is a lollipop-shaped device that is placed on the tongue. It converts visual images into patterns of electrotactile stimulation (the sensation is apparently rather like the taste of battery terminals). Neuroimaging data collected after training showed that the TDU activated the visual cortex of blind subjects. Kupers *et al.* (2006) then used transcranial magnetic stimulation (TMS) to study the sensations experienced by their blind subjects. TMS is a relatively new non-invasive technique to stimulate neural activity in the cortex. A coil is placed close to the scalp and a rapidly changing magnetic field is directed at the cortex below. When directed at the visual cortex of normal sighted subjects, TMS induces 'phosphenes' or flashes of light; visual sensations. Kupers *et al.* (2006) found that when TMS was applied to the visual cortex of the blind subjects they had trained on the TDU, it induced tactile sensations apparently located on the tongue.

How can the source of a sensation apparently overrule its destination? Although sensory cortex is divided into a number of specialized, modality-specific areas, there are reciprocal connections between these areas that allow them to exchange information. These connections mediate some well-known interactions between the senses that are discussed in detail later in Chapter 9. Training on the TDU may have reinforced a pathway linking somatosensory cortex to visual cortex, so that subsequent stimulation of the latter found its way back to the former to provoke a tactile sensation. It is, of course, also unclear what a visual sensation would feel like to a congenitally blind individual in any case. Could they report a visual sensation if they had never experienced one before?

Summary

- Neuropsychological case studies show that specific populations of neurons specialize in conveying information about particular sensory qualities; when those neurons are damaged, perception is compromised in a highly selective manner.
- Brain stimulation and neuroimaging data both reveal that the cortical destination of incoming fibers determines the character of sensations; when you see a light, hear a sound, or feel a touch the appropriate area of cortical tissue is active.
- Single-unit recordings reveal that individual cortical cells are highly specialized, responding only to a narrow range of stimuli within a particular sensory modality. The spatial arrangement of cortical cells within the cortical tissue is very highly ordered according to stimulus preference.
- Functional specialization is a key feature at all levels of every sensory system.

REFLECTIVE EXERCISE

1. Cortical magnification refers to:
   a. Examination of the brain in a microscope
   b. Distorted mapping from a receptive surface to the brain
   c. Enhanced responses found in neuroimaging
   d. A clinical disorder

2. Critically assess the inferences that one can draw about sensory processing from individual clinical case studies.

3. Evaluate and compare the ethical issues raised by the different research techniques that have been used to study sensory function in the brain.

FURTHER READING

- Barlow, H.B. (1982) David Hubel and Torsten Wiesel: their contribution towards understanding the primary visual cortex. *Trends in Neurosciences, 5,* 145–152.

- Calvin, W.H., & Ojemann, G.A. (1994) *Conversations with Neil's Brain: The Neural Nature of Thought and Language.* New York: Addison-Wesley.
- Farah, M.J. (2004) *Visual Agnosia.* Second Edition. Cambridge, MA: MIT Press.
- Guldin, W.O., & Grusser, O.-J. (1998) Is there a vestibular cortex? *Trends in Neurosciences*, *21*, 254–259.

Psychophysics

4

What this chapter will teach you

- What is psychophysics?
- What do absolute thresholds measure?
- What do differential thresholds measure?
- How useful is the notion of a 'window of detectability'?
- What does selective adaptation reveal about perception?

Introduction

Modern researchers can avail themselves of a whole battery of sophisticated physiological techniques for studying the sensory systems, as you saw in the previous chapter, but 150 years ago options for studying the human sensory systems were much more limited. Clinical case histories provided some behavioral clues, but detailed information about tissue damage in these cases had to wait until post-mortem examination. Researchers understood that perception depended on the action of the nervous system, but they had to rely on more indirect methods to study sensory function, in which perceptual responses played a crucial role. These methods are the cornerstone of an area of research known as **psychophysics**. They supply scientific tools for studying the relation between physical stimuli and perceptual experience. The foundations of psychophysical methods, and indeed of the whole scientific discipline of experimental psychology, were laid by two professors at Leipzig University in the middle of the nineteenth century, named Ernst Weber and Gustav Fechner.

Weber and Fechner

E.H. Weber was a physiologist, and G.T. Fechner was a physicist (who studied anatomy under Weber while taking a medical degree at the age of 16). Weber had been recording subjects' judgments of lifted weights, and noticed a pattern: in order for a weight to be just noticeably different from a preceding weight, the change in weight always had to be a constant fraction of the original weight. To give a specific example, let's say that you have a 1000 gram weight in your hand and in order for it to feel just noticeably heavier an additional 50 grams must be added. So the **just noticeable difference (JND)** is 50 grams. How much additional weight would be needed if the original weight was 2000 grams? Weber's observations indicated that it would have to be 100 grams. Similarly the JND for a 4000 gram weight would be 200 grams. Psychophysical experiments that measure JNDs for weight bear out Weber's observations, at least for moderate weights (Ross & Brodie, 1987). Notice that the JND is not a constant arithmetic difference between the weights, but a constant *fraction* of 1/20. **Weber's Law**, as it is known, is a general feature of all the sensory systems (within limits). In order for a sensory stimulus, whether a weight, a light, or a sound, to change by a noticeably different amount, it must change in magnitude by a constant fraction of its original value, known as the **Weber fraction**. Weber fractions across the sensory systems tend to vary between 1/100 and 1/12, or 1% and 8% (Teghtsoonian, 1971).

Fechner went a critical step farther than Weber. Starting from the initial detection of a very weak stimulus (a tiny weight, a dim light), he reasoned that if you were to count

Key Terms

Psychophysics. The scientific study of the relation between physical stimulation and perceptual experience.

Just noticeable difference (JND). The smallest change in sensory stimulation that can be reliably detected by an experimental participant, measured using a psychophysical method.

Weber's Law. The principle that the JND is a constant fraction of the initial stimulus value.

Weber fraction. The constant fractional value associated with a JND.

up just noticeable differences in stimulus intensity you would actually be counting up equal sensory intervals along a subjective, psychological scale of perceived magnitude. So a small increment to a light weight (or a dim light, or a quiet sound) would produce

Key Term

Fechner's Law. A principle describing the relationship between sensation magnitude and stimulus magnitude.

the same increase in perceived weightiness (or brightness or loudness) as a large increment to a very heavy weight (or a bright light, or a loud sound). This insight became known as **Fechner's Law**, and it had a fundamental impact on psychology and physiology. It offered the beginnings of an answer to an age-old philosophical problem, the relation between mind and body, the mental (psychical) world and the physical world. Fechner had discovered a simple mathematical link between the laws of the mind and the laws of physics; a *psychophysical* law. He went on to work out and formalize a set of psychophysical methods for measuring JNDs. Variants of these methods are still in use today to measure both JNDs and other more complex psychophysical phenomena, and they still yield insights about sensory function that could not be obtained by any other means.

KEY CONCEPT

Psychophysical threshold

In *Elemente der Psychophysik*, published in 1860, Fechner described several experimental methods to measure the relation between sensory stimuli and perceptual responses, and these methods have been refined over the years to improve their reliability. As an example, consider a simple 'yes/no' psychophysical method to measure the relation between stimulus intensity and detection. The participant is presented with a stimulus, and asked to respond 'yes' or 'no' to indicate whether they can detect it or not. How heavy (or loud, or bright) must the stimulus be for the participant to detect it? A typical experiment might run as follows. The participant is given a series of trials, each of which contains a stimulus, but stimulus intensity is selected at random from a set of alternative possible values. In each trial the participant is asked to respond 'yes' if they detected the stimulus, or 'no' if they did not. The probability of detection depends on stimulus intensity, usually in the way depicted in Figure 4.1. At low intensities the stimulus is hardly ever detected, while at high intensities it is nearly always detected. The relationship shown in Figure 4.1 is known as a psychometric function. The smooth shape of the function means that there is no single stimulus intensity at which one can say that the stimulus suddenly becomes detectable. Nevertheless experimenters usually want to produce a single figure to represent the participant's sensitivity to the stimulus, so that they can compare sensitivity in different conditions. The convention is to take the stimulus value at the halfway point of the function, corresponding to 50% detection, as the measure of sensitivity, and this is known as the detection threshold.

A major concern in yes/no tasks is how participants handle uncertainty. When the participant is unsure and feels that they are guessing, there are several ways in which they can deal with the uncertainty. They may be conservative, and say 'yes' only when they are absolutely sure that they have detected something. On the other hand they may be liberal, and say 'yes' when they get only the slightest hint that a stimulus is present. They may even have a socially conditioned predisposition against saying 'no', and therefore say 'yes' more often than the sensory information warrants. All of these response strategies are liable to introduce some bias in the estimate of threshold, shifting the measured curve or changing its slope. Psychophysicists now use experimental designs and analysis techniques that aim to separate out bias effects from sensitivity effects. One simple way to encourage unbiased responses is to avoid 'yes/no' discriminations. Each trial contains two stimulus intervals, separated either in time or in space, only one of which contains the stimulus. The participant responds '1' or '2' (or 'left' or 'right') to denote the interval in which they detected a stimulus. At low intensities the participant can only guess which interval contained the stimulus, so the probability of a correct response is near 50%; at sufficiently high intensities the discrimination is relatively easy, so performance is near-perfect. This technique is called two-alternative forced choice, or 2AFC for short. Unlike a yes/no task, in a 2AFC task the participant *always* has to choose one or the other stimulus interval, so bias introduced by their (un) willingness to commit to detection is not a problem (Green & Swets, 1966). The psychometric function produced by a 2AFC task necessarily varies between 50% and 100%, rather than the 0% to 100% range in Figure 4.1, and threshold is defined as the 75% point of the curve.

As described, the 2AFC method measures absolute threshold. Only one of the two intervals contains a stimulus, and the method finds the minimum absolute amount of stimulation needed to achieve 75% correct discrimination between the empty and filled intervals. The 2AFC method can also be used to measure JNDs. In this case both intervals contain stimuli. One stimulus remains fixed in value (though it is randomly presented in either one interval or the other), and the other stimulus varies along some dimension such as loudness, brightness, or whatever. The participant's task is to select the interval containing the louder, brighter, or whatever stimulus. The 75% point of the resulting psychometric function defines the JND, sometimes called the differential threshold.

Psychophysical experiments offer answers to many questions about the sensory systems with reliable, accurate perceptual data. To give just a few examples:

- How quickly does your sensitivity to light change when you are placed in the dark?
- How does your ability to discriminate touch vary across the body surface?
- How does visual acuity vary across the visual field?
- How does sensory adaptation alter your sensitivity?

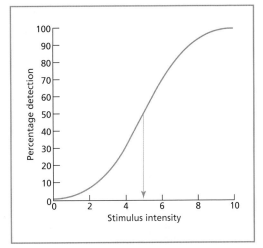

Figure 4.1 Typical results of a psychophysical detection experiment. When the intensity of the stimulus is low, the participant cannot reliably detect it, so performance is near zero. As intensity increases, performance climbs to near-perfect detection. The threshold is conventionally defined as the stimulus intensity yielding 50% detection (arrow).

The answers to questions such as these can be related to the known physiological properties of the sensory systems, if one makes a basic assumption about the link between sensations and neural activity: When two stimuli produce discriminably different sensory impressions, they *must* produce different patterns of neural activity in the sensory system. If this assumption holds, then the converse must also be true: Perceptually indistinguishable stimuli *must* produce identical (or near-identical) neural responses. If one accepts this assumption, then perceptual discriminability can be used as a proxy for neural discriminability. Psychophysical experiments can therefore reveal something about the underlying neural processes.

Thresholds

Absolute threshold

Most people are familiar with the experience of entering a theater after the performance has started. The sudden darkness causes temporary blindness, and you need help to find your seat. Vision gradually returns after a short while. This process is known as dark adaptation, and it can be measured psychophysically (see Pirenne, 1962). The solid line in Figure 4.2 shows how the absolute threshold for detecting a small spot of light changes over time after the participant has been placed in the dark. The threshold falls gradually over a period of about 20 minutes, so the participant becomes progressively more sensitive

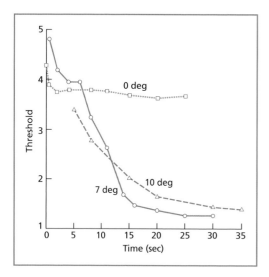

Figure 4.2 The time course of dark adaptation. Solid line: absolute threshold for detecting a small light spot measured while looking slightly away from the light; dotted line: threshold while looking directly at the spot; dashed line: threshold while looking well away from the spot.

to very faint lights. This process mirrors the reappearance of vision in the dark theater. There is a revealing hiccup in the curve at around 7 minutes. Dark adaptation seems to stall, and then take off again. This kind of curve is obtained when the spot is placed just to one side of the participant's line of sight. If the participant looks directly at the spot, the threshold curve shown by the dotted line is obtained; it follows the early part of the solid curve. If the participant looks well away from the spot while performing the experiment, the dashed threshold curve is obtained; this follows the late part of the solid curve. This pattern of data can be explained using the known properties of the photoreceptors, which were outlined in Chapter 1. Cone photoreceptors function well only in bright conditions, while rod photoreceptors function only in dark conditions. Furthermore, cones are confined to the central area of the retina, while rods are most plentiful out in the periphery of the retina. Now the origin of the curves in Figure 4.2 becomes clear. When participants look directly at the spot they see it using only cones, so there is little scope for dark adaptation (the dotted curve). When participants look well away from the spot they see it using only rods, so dark adaptation allows them to see at very dim luminances (the dashed curve). When participants look just slightly away from the spot, they use an area of the retina that contains both rods and cones, so the dark adaptation curve includes contributions from both; the early part is mediated by cones and the late part is mediated by rods. There is a glitch at the transition between them, known as the rod–cone break.

In general, psychophysical studies of absolute sensitivity are very informative about the state of the sensory receptors, and can be used as a diagnostic tool. For instance, dark adaptation in individuals who lack cone photoreceptors completely does not show the rod–cone break, but always follows the dashed curve in

DISCUSS AND DEBATE

You may have noticed that the world appears a little murky and hazy at dusk. This reflects the fact that dark adaptation is not complete, and neither class of photoreceptor is operating at peak efficiency; your visual system has reached the rod–cone break.

Figure 4.2 (Rushton, 1961). Psychophysical studies of hearing also show that the absolute threshold for sound gradually rises with age (Morrell *et al.*, 1996); we become hard of hearing, and this can be related to deterioration in the cochlear hair cells.

Differential threshold

The threshold for discriminating small differences in touch can be measured using a pair of calipers (as shown at the top of Figure 4.3). Either one or both points of the calipers are placed on the skin, and a blindfolded participant is asked to report whether they feel a single point or two points. When the gap between the points is very small participants perform at chance; they cannot tell the difference between one and two points. The differential threshold estimates the smallest point separation that can be reliably discriminated by the participant. The graph in Figure 4.3 shows thresholds obtained on different parts of the body (Weinstein, 1968). At some locations, notably the tongue and fingers, the discrimination threshold is very small; around 2 or 3 mm. At other locations such as on the back or neck the threshold is very much worse, at around 60 mm. Why are there such dramatic variations in sensitivity around the body? Refer back to Penfield's map of somatosensory cortex, shown in Figure 3.4. There is a much greater area of sensory cortex devoted to the tongue and fingers than there is devoted to the neck and back. Furthermore the receptive fields of cortical neurons in the finger area are very much smaller, at around 1–2 mm, than those in the back area (somatosensory receptive fields were illustrated in Figure 2.3).

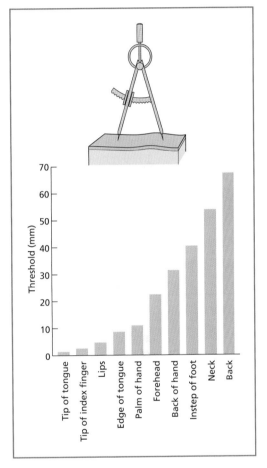

Figure 4.3 Differential threshold for touch, measured using calipers (top). Either one or both tips touch the skin, and the participant must discriminate between the two sensations. The graph (bottom) shows the minimum separation between the tips in order for reliable discrimination, in different parts of the body.

Therefore in the area of cortex devoted to the fingers, a separation between the caliper points of 2–3 mm is likely to excite different neurons, and evoke distinct sensory impressions of the two points. In the area of cortex devoted to the back, on the other hand, the separation must be very much larger in order to excite different neurons and so create discriminable sensations.

In a similar way, visual acuity for spatial detail is very much higher at the center of the retina than out in the periphery. You can read the one or two words you are looking at directly, but not the words beyond that. This decline in visual acuity is due to the cortical magnification evident in Figure 3.4, and the corresponding variation in visual receptive field size at different retinal locations (Anstis, 1998).

Limits of sensory detection

Humans can detect light wavelengths only within a narrow band of the full electromagnetic spectrum extending from about 400 nm to 700 nm, as you discovered in Chapter 1 (p. 12). Wavelengths outside this range are invisible, so it defines a window through which we can see the world. The idea of a window of sensory detectability can be applied to other stimulus dimensions across all the sensory modalities. The limits can be related to sensory physiology, and to the ecological niche in which humans evolved. Furthermore, if the limits of sensory detection are known, then equipment such as visual displays and audio systems can be designed so that they are optimally matched to human capacities and, equally important, information that can never be detected can be discarded. The limits of detection in hearing and vision have been explored in the most depth, so they are described in detail in the following sections.

Window of audibility

In audition the absolute threshold for detecting a sound depends on its frequency (see Chapter 1 for an explanation of sound frequency). Figure 4.4 shows the window of audibility (Moore, 1997). The horizontal axis is sound frequency, in hertz (Hz). The vertical axis is sound level. The oval shape shows the borders of the window; sounds inside the window are loud enough to be heard safely, while sounds outside the window are inaudible or dangerous. The lower border shows the minimum sound

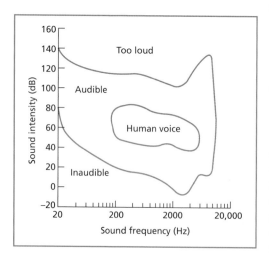

Figure 4.4 Window of detectability for audition. The outer oval marks the border between sounds that are too quiet to be heard, or too loud to be safely received. The inner oval marks the range of frequencies in the human voice. Based on Mather (2009) and Wolfe *et al.* (2006).

level needed for detection, and the upper border shows the maximum sound level that can be sustained without pain and damage. Notice that frequencies below about 20 Hz and above 20 kHz cannot be heard at all, whatever their sound level. Sound frequencies in the human voice are well matched to the window of audibility; they pass through the middle of the window, presumably as a consequence of evolution. Some animals produce sounds that do not pass through the human window: Elephant calls have a frequency that falls below the lower frequency limit of the window, known as infra-sound (Garstang, 2004); bat echolocation calls have a frequency that is well above the upper limit of the window, known as ultrasound (Neuweiler, 1984).

The limited range of frequencies audible to humans has important practical applications. You take advantage of the window of audibility every time you convert or transfer an MP3 audio file. There is no point in occupying storage space and transmission bandwidth with audio information that humans cannot perceive. So the compression algo-rithm used in the MP3 format discards sound frequencies that fall outside the window of audibility.

Window of visibility

Changes in image intensity over space and over time are particularly important for vision. Changes over space convey information about spatial features (edges, bars, lines). Changes over time reveal move-ment, because moving bars or edges cause parts of the image to lighten or darken momentarily as they move past. However our ability to detect both kinds of intensity change is limited. Psychophysical experiments that measure the ability to detect repetitive change over space use grating patterns that alternate between bright and dark bars. The fineness of the bars in a grating is usually specified in terms of the number of dark–light cycles per degree (cpd) of **visual angle** (usually called **spatial frequency**). Low frequency gratings have broad bars and high frequency gratings have thin, closely spaced bars. The fingers of your outstretched hand at arm's length create a grating pattern with a spatial frequency of about 0.25 cpd. There is a limit to a human observer's ability to resolve the bars in grat-ings. Grating patterns above about 40 cycles per degree usually cannot be resolved at all, and instead appear to be

Key Terms

Visual angle. A unit of measurement specifying how large the image of an object is at the retina, based on the angle it subtends; see Figure 1.7.

Spatial frequency. Standard measure of the fineness of the bars in a grating pattern, which corresponds to the number of dark–light cycles per unit of visual angle (per degree).

Key Term

Temporal frequency. Standard measure of flicker rate in a visual stimulus, which corresponds to the number of on–off cycles per second, measured in hertz (Hz).

uniform (Campbell & Robson, 1968). This spatial frequency limit corresponds to viewing the millimeter markings on a ruler from a distance of 2.29 meters. Beyond that distance, a typical observer will not be able to make out the individual markings.

Psychophysical measurements of sensitivity to temporal change in vision use lights that flicker rapidly between bright and dark. The rate of flicker is specified in terms of **temporal frequency**, measured in hertz (Hz). Automotive indicators flash at between 1 and 2 Hz. Human ability to see flicker extends to quite high frequencies, but is limited to frequencies below about 50 Hz (de Lange, 1958). Above that frequency the flickering light appears to be steady.

Figure 4.5 summarizes the window of visibility for vision, including both spatial and temporal limits (Kelly, 1966). The vertical axis plots spatial frequency, and the horizontal axis plots temporal frequency. Combinations of spatial and temporal frequency (flickering spatial patterns) that lie inside the outer border can be seen, while combinations outside the border are invisible to a human. We are most sensitive to medium spatial and temporal frequencies, shown by the inner oval shape.

The data in Figure 4.5 show that you can see visual detail only when its spatial or temporal variation falls within the window of visibility. These limits can be exploited to minimize the size of digital images and movies, which can occupy quite a lot of storage space, and take a long time to download. As in the case of MP3 audio files, there is no point in a file containing spatial detail or temporal information that is beyond the limits of human capabilities (at a normal viewing distance). So image file formats such as JPEG throw away some detail to minimize file size while retaining an acceptable appearance.

The window of visibility can also be used deliberately to place information *beyond* the visible range. Room and street lights, computer and television displays, all flicker at 50 or 60 Hz (it varies between countries) so that they appear to be

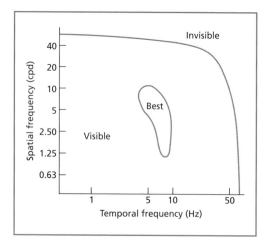

Figure 4.5 Window of detectability for vision. Spatial and temporal variations beyond the outer line are too fine and/or rapid to be seen. The inner oval marks the spatial and temporal variations that are most easily seen.

continuously illuminated even though they are not. These temporal frequencies lie outside the window of sensibility.

RESEARCH QUESTION

Does subliminal advertising and messaging work?

In the late 1950s an advertising executive named James Vicary caused an outcry in the USA when he claimed that a subliminal advertisement screened during a film had led to a sudden increase in the sales of popcorn and Coke in the theater. In his study Vicary claimed to have secretly flashed the words 'Eat popcorn' and 'Drink Coke' on the movie screen for a third of a millisecond, every five seconds during the film. The outcry led to a US ban on 'subliminal advertising'. However no scientific report of the study was ever published, and it turns out that the study was almost certainly fabricated. Nor has anyone successfully replicated the effect. Nevertheless, a belief in the effectiveness of subliminal advertising has become firmly established among the general public.

Recent research actually does offer qualified support for the belief. Karremans et al. (2006) presented the brand name of a drink subliminally during an irrelevant visual detection task, before measuring participants' preference for different drink brands. They found that the subliminal presentation did significantly affect participants' tendency to select a particular brand, but only among thirsty participants. Karremans et al. (2006) reported that a second set of control participants were unable to guess the brand name that was presented during the task, supporting their contention that the presentation really was subliminal, though they presented no details of this crucial control experiment. More recently Bermeitinger et al. (2009) found that a subliminally presented brand name influenced actual consumption, but again the effect was confined to participants in the appropriate need-related motivational state (in this case, the use of dextrose pills to alleviate tiredness and maintain concentration). Bermeitinger et al. (2009) also gave details of control measurements to confirm that participants were not aware of the subliminal brand names.

The 1980s and 1990s saw another manifestation of this belief in the power of subliminal messages, in the form of self-help audio tapes that claimed to improve memory, self-esteem, weight control, and smoking behavior. The

Key Term

Subliminal stimulus. A sensory stimulus that is too weak to be consciously perceived but may nevertheless influence perception, cognition, or action.

subliminal messages were hidden in tapes that appeared to contain only relaxing sounds such as music or natural sounds. Greenwald *et al.* (1991) tested the effectiveness of two such tapes using an experiment in which 288 volunteers who were interested in improving their memory or self-esteem followed the manufacturers' instructions and listened to a tape for a month. In a double-blind design, half of the volunteers who believed they were listening to a memory self-help tape actually listened to a self-esteem tape, and vice versa. Independent tests of memory and self-esteem were administered before and after the volunteers used the tapes. The results showed no significant change in memory or self-esteem associated with administration of the appropriate tape. There was, however, some improvement in memory or self-esteem irrespective of the particular tape used, which one might attribute to a placebo or practice effect.

Subliminal perception is not so far-fetched. As you have seen in this chapter, a sensory threshold is not an all-or-nothing phenomenon; there is a gradual, statistical shift from one perceptual experience to the other across the threshold. There are also many scientifically rigorous studies which show that subliminal information can influence perception. For example, there is a well-known effect called subthreshold summation, in which two sensory stimuli that are not detectable individually can combine to produce a suprathreshold effect. Subthreshold summation only occurs using similar stimuli, and is thought to be caused by stimulus energy being summed in neurons that are sensitive to both stimuli. However the claims of subliminal advertising and self-help tapes go much further than simple subliminal summation. They claim that information which does not produce a conscious experience can actually influence behavior in significant ways. Recent evidence supports the claim that subliminal advertising may influence brand choices in appropriately motivated individuals, but offers no support for claims about the effectiveness of self-help tapes.

Adaptation

Everyone has first-hand experience of fluctuations in their sensory impressions after prolonged exposure to a particular sensory environment. The cooking smell lingering in your house disappears after a while; the itch from a shirt fabric fades away as you wear it; the pink tinge induced by your sunglasses becomes less noticeable. These changes are mostly happening inside your head, not in the world; if you leave the house for a while and then return, the cooking smell reappears. They are all examples of sensory adaptation, which can be measured psychophysically. Adaptation affects not only the perceived intensity of a stimulus, but also its appearance. One of the oldest known after-effects of adaptation was first noticed by the Greek philosopher Aristotle in 330 BC, and is known as the **motion after-effect (MAE**; Mather *et al.*, 1998). It is one of the most robust and easily demonstrated of all adaptation effects.

The strength of the MAE can be measured using a variant of the 2AFC paradigm described earlier in the chapter. In each trial the participant is briefly shown a test pattern that contains dots moving in many different directions. In some trials a proportion of the dots move consistently in one direction or the opposite. Let's say that the two directions are up and down. Figure 4.6 (top) shows example stimuli. After each presentation the participant's task is to report the movement direction of the dots (up versus down). A typical psychometric function from this task is shown by the solid line in the graph (Blake & Hiris, 1993). 'Up' responses predominate when some of the dots move up, 'down' responses predominate when they move down, and responses are near to 50% when there are few or no dots moving in either direction. Here the 50% point is of particular interest, sometimes called the **point of subjective equality (PSE)** because it represents the point at which the participant is equally disposed toward the two alternative responses.

Now if the task is performed after the participant has adapted to a pattern that contains strong upward motion, the psychometric function looks rather different. As the dashed line in Figure 4.6 shows, the function is shifted to the right relative to the first function. Notice that when there is no consistent physical motion in the stimulus (zero on the horizontal axis) there is a preponderance of downward responses; the pattern appears to move downward, reflecting the MAE. In order for the test pattern to appear stationary, just enough

> ## DISCUSS AND DEBATE
>
> The motion after-effect can easily be observed when watching television. While the credits scroll up the screen at the end of a program, fixate a stationary point on the television. Any stationary image that immediately follows the credits will appear to move downwards. Steady fixation is essential, because tracking eye movements necessarily destroy the retinal motion, and any adaptation is very specific to the area of retina exposed to the moving pattern.

Key Terms

Motion after-effect (MAE). Following adaptation to visual movement in a particular direction, a stationary pattern appears to move in the opposite direction.

Point of subjective equality (PSE). The 50% point of a psychometric function, at which the participant is equally disposed toward two alternative responses.

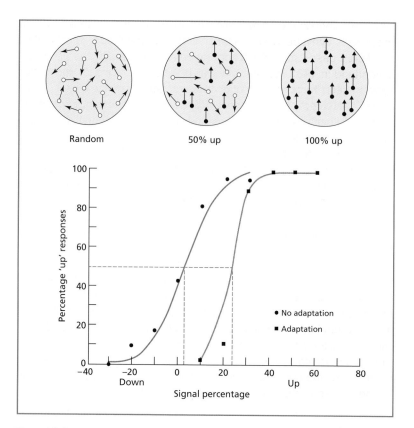

Random   50% up   100% up

Figure 4.6 Results of an experiment to measure the strength of the motion after-effect. The test stimulus contains a variable proportion of dots moving consistently upwards or downwards (top). Prior to adaptation (blue line, circles), the 50% point of the psychometric function corresponds to a randomly moving pattern (zero on the horizontal axis). After adapting to upward motion (purple line, squares) the random pattern appears to move down, so a stimulus at zero on the horizontal axis produces only 'down' responses (i.e. no 'up' responses). Some upwards dots have to be added to cancel out this apparent movement, shown by the shift in the 50% point. Reprinted from Blake and Hiris (1993), copyright 1993, with permission from Elsevier.

upward motion has to be added to counteract or null out the apparent motion produced by the MAE. The physical motion that is needed to produce an apparently stationary test pattern (as defined by the participant's PSE) is a measure of the strength of the after-effect.

Not only is the MAE easy to demonstrate and to measure, but it also has a well-established explanation. Recall from the previous chapter that many cortical cells are selectively responsive to the direction of stimulus motion, though they still produce a relatively small response in the presence of stationary stimuli. The discovery of these cells by Hubel and Wiesel (1959) soon inspired an explanation for MAE based on visual physiology, first described by Stuart Sutherland in 1961 (Sutherland, 1961). The direction in which something is seen to move depends on the relative activity in cells tuned to different directions. After prolonged exposure to motion in a particular direction, a stationary image produces less activity than normal in the cells that had been stimulated, so apparent movement in the opposite direction is seen. At the time this explanation was first proposed, no one had directly observed adaptation-induced changes in neural activity, but many papers have since reported neural adaptation that is consistent with the explanation (e.g. Hammond *et al.*, 1985).

The MAE convincingly illustrates just how tightly coupled are sensory experiences and neural activity. Changes in the balance of activation across cells tuned to different stimuli have direct consequences for perception. Selective tuning is a universal feature of sensory neurons, and psychophysical measurement of adaptation effects is a well-established and reliable tool for investigating it. In the auditory domain, the apparent location of a sound source can be shifted by adaptation. Recall from the previous chapter that one source of information about the direction from which a sound emanates is the difference in the time of arrival of the sound between the two ears. For instance, when the sound arrives at the right ear less than one thousandth of a second before it arrives at the left ear, the sound is perceived to be emanating from toward the right-hand side of space. Kashino and Nishida (1998) presented auditory stimuli with various inter-aural time differences to participants using a 2AFC procedure. After each presentation the participant reported whether the sound appeared to be localized on the left or on the right. Prior to adaptation, direction reports showed no bias in favor of either direction. After adapting to a sound with an inter-aural time difference corresponding to, say, a rightward direction, responses were biased in favor of a leftward direction. This auditory analog of many visual after-effects can be explained by supposing that the auditory system contains cells that are selectively tuned to specific inter-aural time differences. Adaptation to any one time difference reduces the responsiveness of the corresponding cells, so biasing activity (and therefore perception) in favor of directions on the opposite side of the head. Cells selectively sensitive to inter-aural time difference have been found in the brains of many animals (e.g. Fitzpatrick et al., 1997; Figure 6.3). The after-effect reported by Kashino and Nishida (1998) indicates that humans possess these cells as well.

A great many other instances of perceptual adaptation have been discovered. Adaptation in the senses of taste and smell seems to be particularly rapid, and is sometimes called habituation. A universal feature of all these effects is their selectivity. Adaptation to a particular stimulus only affects perception of similar stimuli. Stimulus selectivity is a key feature of sensory physiology, so psychophysical adaptation effects show just how closely perception is tied to physiology.

Evaluation

The psychophysical methods that grew from the work of Weber and Fechner have led to some crucial discoveries about the human sensory systems, discoveries that would not have been possible using any other method. Psychophysics provides tools to study the sensitivity and stimulus selectivity of cells in the human sensory systems non-invasively, using no more than some carefully created stimuli, a response recording device, and a cooperative (if occasionally bored) experimental participant.

Theories derived from psychophysical data have been profoundly influenced by anatomical and physiological knowledge. Before the development of single-unit recording techniques psychophysical theories were inspired by anatomy (Lashley *et al.*, 1951). The anatomical uniformity of the cerebral cortex led people to believe that neural function was also uniform. Theorists believed that perception was mediated by large-scale patterns of activity across the entire cortex, rather than responses in small groups of cells. When single-unit recordings revealed that individual cells were highly specialized in terms of their stimulus preferences, new psychophysical theories emerged in which perception was said to depend on the relative activity of comparatively small populations of detectors tuned to different stimuli (as in the explanation for the MAE). An extreme version of this theoretical perspective posited individual cells that were able to encode the identity of a complex entity such as your grandmother, or a Volkswagen car (Gross, 2002). These early theories were limited because they lacked a broad theoretical perspective that took into account the tasks performed by the sensory systems, and the problems they faced in completing those tasks. The conceptual framework described in the next chapter supplies the necessary theoretical sophistication.

Summary

- Psychophysics supplies scientific tools for studying the relation between physical stimuli and perceptual experience. They were first developed by Weber and Fechner in the 1800s.
- Absolute thresholds measure the minimum amount of stimulation required for a perceptual response, and provide useful information about the state of sensory receptors.
- Differential thresholds measure the minimum change in stimulation required for a noticeable perceptual change. They identify which stimuli produce the sharpest perceptual discrimination.
- Thresholds can be used to define windows of detectability – the range of stimuli that is capable of producing a perceptual response. Sensory limits can be related to knowledge of the underlying physiology, and can also be used to design efficient information storage and transmission systems.
- Selective adaptation is a universal feature of perception, and is related to the stimulus selectivity of underlying neurons in the sensory systems.

REFLECTIVE EXERCISE

1. According to Weber's Law, two stimuli are discriminable when they differ:
   a.   By a constant fraction
   b.   By a constant difference
   c.   In their absolute thresholds
   d.   In their window of detectability

2. How would you design an experiment to measure the change in the apparent tilt of lines in a pattern induced by adaptation to lines tilted at a nearby orientation (the tilt after-effect)?

3. Evaluate the relevance of sensory thresholds to the design of human interfaces in modern instrumentation such as those in aircraft.

FURTHER READING

- Anstis, S., Verstraten, F.A.J., & Mather, G. (1998) The motion after-effect. *Trends in Cognitive Sciences, 2*, 111–117.
- Gross, C.G. (2002) Genealogy of the 'Grandmother Cell'. *Neuroscientist, 8*, 512–518.
- Kingdom, F.A.A., & Prins, N. (2010) *Psychophysics: A Practical Introduction.* London: Academic Press.
- Mather, G. (2009) *Foundations of Sensation and Perception.* Hove, UK: Psychology Press.
- Stevens, S.S. (1970) Neural events and the psychophysical law. *Science, 170*, 1043–1050.

Perception as information processing

5

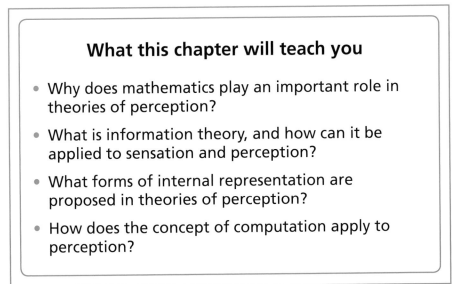

What this chapter will teach you

- Why does mathematics play an important role in theories of perception?
- What is information theory, and how can it be applied to sensation and perception?
- What forms of internal representation are proposed in theories of perception?
- How does the concept of computation apply to perception?

Introduction

So far you have explored sensation and perception from the perspective of several empirical disciplines: Anatomy reveals neural structure, neurophysiology and neuropsychology reveal neural function, and psychophysics reveals sensory and perceptual function. A deeper, more integrated understanding of the human senses requires a solid theoretical framework that unifies these different approaches, a coherent conceptual structure within which specific ideas can be placed and evaluated. Mathematics is the rigorous, universal language that underpins all of the sciences. So it is not surprising that three twentieth-century mathematicians laid the conceptual foundations of all modern scientific theories of perception, and indeed of cognitive psychology as a whole. They were Alan Turing (1912–1954), Claude Shannon (1916–2001), and David Marr (1945–1980). Shannon was an American mathematician from Michigan, while Turing and Marr were Britons who both studied mathematics at Cambridge University (and died tragically young).

Mathematical foundations of cognitive science

The Turing Machine

Turing wrote a series of influential papers on mathematical logic both before and after his highly distinguished service as a code-breaker during the Second World War. He laid the logical and conceptual foundations of modern computers by describing, in abstract terms, a computing device that could manipulate symbols according to a set of rules. At the time this so-called Turing Machine was conceived mathematically as a mechanical device that could read and write symbols on a strip of tape. Arbitrarily complex operations could be performed by chaining together long sequences of simple read and write operations. This theory encapsulated the function of the central processing unit (CPU) in present-day computers, and so described the essence of modern computer science. Turing's device was imaginary, but it has become a reality in today's computers. Let's take a very simple specific example to illustrate the idea. Say you are typing an essay using a computer's word processor, and you decide to capitalize a word that you have typed in. You highlight the word using the mouse interface, and then select the 'All Caps' option in the word processor's on-screen menu. The word becomes capitalized. The operation is performed in modern computers in precisely the way Turing described. Internally all computers store each letter in the alphabet as a number, and different numbers are allocated to lower-case and upper-case versions of each letter. So for 'a', 'b', 'c', 'd', etc. the numbers may be 97, 98, 99, 100, etc., while for 'A', 'B', 'C', 'D', etc. the numbers may be 65, 66, 67, 68, etc. So to capitalize a word the computer executes a series of instructions, part of which do the following:

1 Read the code of the next character in the word stored in the document file.
2 Subtract 32 from the code.
3 Write the new code back into the working document file, replacing the old code.

A crucial aspect of the theory from the point of view of cognitive science was Turing's claim that 'It is possible to invent a single machine which can be used to compute any computable sequence' (Turing, 1936, p. 241). He argued, essentially, that all sufficiently powerful computing devices are identical in the sense that any one of them can emulate the operation of any other. Turing viewed the brain as a kind of computing device. It followed from this argument that a computing machine could be used to simulate human cognition, if it were sufficiently sophisticated. Turing thus established the mathematical basis for computer models of human perception and cognition, long before the invention of modern computers.

Information theory

Around the same time that Turing was developing his ideas about machine intelligence, Claude Shannon was working for a US telecommunications company, and published a paper that provided the first mathematical account of how information is transmitted in a communication system such as a telephone network. Shannon (1948) provided a schematic diagram of a general communications system similar to that shown in Figure 5.1.

Although the scheme was designed to describe the wired telephone network of the 1940s, it is equally applicable to modern cellular phone

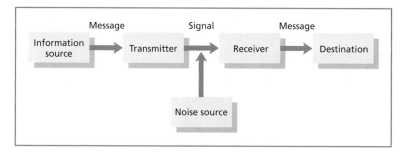

Figure 5.1 Schematic diagram of a communications system, as described by Claude Shannon in 1948.

communications systems. A message emanates from a source, the human operator's voice in this example. A transmitter converts the message into a form suitable for transmission. In cellular phone telephony this corresponds to the conversion of sound pressure into electrical current by a microphone inside the phone. A communications channel (the cellular phone network) then transfers the signal to the receiver (another phone). Here the signal is converted back from electrical current into sound pressure waves by an audio speaker, so reconstructing the original message. The destination is the intended recipient of the phone call.

The message and signal both carry information that can be described mathematically as values that vary over time and/or space (sound pressure, radio signals, or images in the case of television signals). All other components of the system can also be described in mathematical terms, and Shannon's analysis identified several key characteristics that determine the efficiency with which the system can transfer information, including:

- Channel capacity – how many signals can be transmitted simultaneously?
- Transmission rate – how quickly can the system transfer signals?
- **Redundancy** – how much information in the signal needs to be transmitted?
- **Noise** – is there intrusion by information that is unrelated to the signal?

Shannon gave precise mathematical descriptions of each of these characteristics. His analysis showed that one can, for example, separate out the problem of data compression from the problem of optimal transmission and deal with them in isolation. Take redundancy, for instance. Some parts of the signal are bound to be more informative than others, so if a mathematical tool could identify the less informative (more redundant) parts of the signal, one could discard the redundant information and so compress the amount of information that needs to be transmitted, improving the efficiency of the system as a whole. For example:

The redundancy of ordinary English, not considering statistical structure over greater distances than about eight letters, is roughly 50%. This means that when we

Key Terms

Redundancy. A term used to describe signal components that add little, if anything, to the information content of a signal.

Noise. Information in a transmission system that is unrelated to the signal, and serves to make the signal more difficult to decipher.

write English half of what we write is determined by the structure of the language and half is chosen freely.

(Shannon, 1948, p. 392)

So one could, in principle, discard approximately 50% of the signal by appropriate encoding of an English message. Many people take advantage of this kind of redundancy when they leave out certain letters while composing text messages (Almst any wrd cn b abbrvted in ths wy).

Information theory is a cornerstone of modern information technology; the huge bandwidth (transmission capacity) of modern cell phone, cable, and internet networks is largely a result of the savings made possible by the application of information theory. It also had a profound impact on cognitive science. For example, you saw in the previous chapter how psychophysics can identify which parts of a sensory signal are visible to a human, and which parts are invisible (windows of detectability). Information theory provides a rigorous functional framework within which one can assess the significance of such psychophysical limits on performance. Armed with information theory it is possible to ask whether the sensory systems have evolved to discard certain signals because they largely carry redundant information.

Psychologists realized that functional diagrams similar to Shannon's (Figure 5.1) could be drawn for the human sensory systems. They capture an abstract, functional description of how the system works, breaking it down into its component parts (Figure 5.2). Source data from the outside world is converted into electrical form by a sense organ (transmitter) and transferred along neural pathways (communications channel) to the cortex (receiver), where it evokes a sensory experience (destination). Information theory supplies mathematical tools that can be

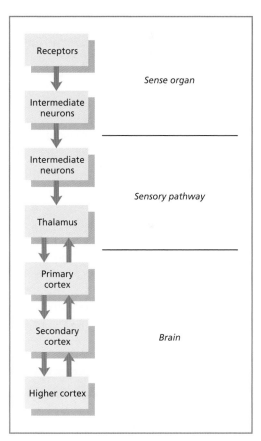

Figure 5.2 Schematic diagram of sensory processing, inspired by Claude Shannon's information theory.

used to analyze the functional properties of sensory systems both at a coarse scale (a whole sensory pathway), and at a fine scale (individual neurons). Moreover, given Turing's insights about universal computers, one could actually design a machine to simulate perception, as follows:

1 Describe the components of the sensory system in abstract functional terms (as in Figure 5.2).
2 Establish the precise mathematical characteristics of the system by applying concepts from information theory to the physiological and psychophysical data.
3 Embody the system in a computer program.

One can assess the adequacy of the simulation as an account of perception by submitting novel sensory stimuli to the computer and recording its output. New psychophysical experiments can then test whether real sensory systems (human observers) produce the same output. Computer models to simulate cognition were first devised in the late 1950s to study human problem solving (Newell & Simon, 1961), though their approach was rather abstract and did not address issues of sensory coding.

Marr's computational theory of vision

Information theory showed that new insights into perception can be gained by viewing it as an information processing task. David Marr adopted this approach wholeheartedly in his book *Vision*, published posthumously in 1982, which set out his detailed computational theory of vision. While working in Cambridge, UK, Marr had initially been captivated by physiology – 'Truth, I believed, was basically neural' (1982, p. 14) – and he developed a computational theory of the **cerebellar cortex** that was closely tied to its physiological properties. However he became dissatisfied with this kind of theory. He wanted to know:

What are the visual areas of the cerebral cortex actually doing? What are the problems in doing it that need explaining, and at what level of description should such explanations be sought?

(1982, p. 15)

Key Term

Cerebellar cortex. A large, complex structure thought to be crucial for the unconscious control of movement, posture, and balance.

Moreover, he felt that the best way of discovering the difficulty of doing something was to try to do it himself.

Simulating perception using a computer

Marr moved to MIT in the USA, where there were powerful computers that he could use to simulate visual processing. In this way he (and others subsequently) discovered that the processing problems posed by perception are formidably difficult to solve using a computer. Even nowadays autonomous guided vehicles are still severely limited in their capabilities compared to a typical human driver (Seetharaman et al., 2006). It turns out that incoming visual data are inherently ambiguous, and do not contain sufficient information on their own to arrive at a unique, and correct, interpretation of the visual scene. Autonomous vehicles supplement visual information with data from radar, lasers, GPS, and maps. Until very recently this information was not available to human drivers, yet we (largely) function very well without it. How do humans manage so well in the face of ambiguous sensory data that admit so many different interpretations? Marr was one of the first to see clearly that the range of possible solutions can be reduced by applying assumptions or constraints based on the properties of the real world. For example, ambiguity in the interpretation of movement in the retinal image can be resolved using an assumption that 'most of the structures in the visual world are rigid, or at least nearly so' (Marr, 1982, p. 209). The rigidity assumption allows a mathematical solution to the otherwise intractable problem of inferring object structure from information about movement (Ullman, 1984).

This do-it-yourself approach to building and testing theories by implementing them on a computer is one of Marr's enduring legacies. It is now taken for granted that a rigorous theory of perception should be couched in detailed computational terms that make its constraints and assumptions explicit. It should be possible to implement the model on a computer so that its performance can be assessed.

Marr's levels of description

A second major contribution relates to Marr's comment above on levels of description. His theory of the cerebellum proposed that it was a simple, powerful memorizing device for learning motor skills. However Marr was not satisfied with the theory because it did not tell him how to build a machine capable of movement. In order to do that, he argued, he needed to know what task the cerebellum performs, at an abstract level. Why does the cerebellum require a memory, and what should the memory contain? Marr believed that knowledge of neural structures alone cannot answer these questions about function. He went on to argue that a full understanding of the cerebellum, or of an area of sensory cortex, requires a new level of description, one that is remote from the neural implementation. He drew an analogy with the computers that make international airline reservations. To understand them fully, it is important to understand the hardware implementation – the computers with their processors, memory, instruction sets, and communications protocols. It is also essential to know something about the task they perform at a more abstract level – to understand aircraft, geography, time zones, fares, flight connections, and so on. So he argued that the problem of perception must be analyzed at an abstract level. One needs to ask: What is the goal of perception? What problem does it solve? What constraints or assumptions does the sensory system apply to reach a solution? The answers to these questions must, of course, relate to the neural implementation, but the link, Marr argued, is very loose. A given solution could, in principle, be implemented in a variety of different neural structures.

Hierarchical processing in perception

Marr's emphasis on an abstract, functional analysis of perception was novel and hugely influential. He argued that the purpose of vision was 'building a description of the shapes and positions of things from images' (1982, p. 36). His theoretical model of how the brain constructs this description divided vision into three hierarchical stages of processing, illustrated in Figure 5.3. At each stage the visual system builds an internal representation of certain properties of the image. In the first stage (local features) the system represents significant local intensity changes (edges, bars, blobs) and their distribution. In the intermediate stage (shape representation) the system represents larger scale structures corresponding to visible surfaces in the image. At the highest stage (object representation) the system represents the objects present in the image, in a form that is suitable for recognition.

This broad three-stage process still attracts wide acceptance in the vision

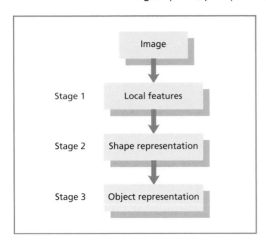

Figure 5.3 Three stages of visual processing, according to David Marr's theory of vision.

community. It is consistent with clinical cases of individuals with brain damage in secondary areas of visual cortex. Such patients generally have a near-normal ability to detect local features such as color, depth, motion, and spatial detail (stage 1 in Figure 5.3), but seem to have a deficit in higher level integrative processes (either in stage 2 or in stage 3 of the processing hierarchy). They can see, but they do not know what they are looking at (see Farah, 2004, for a review).

Some patients cannot name, copy, or match even simple shapes. A triangle, for instance, is confused with a circle. They seem to have a deficit in stage 2 of processing, a condition known as **apperceptive agnosia**. Other patients are able to copy and match shapes normally, but cannot identify objects from their images. They seem to have a deficit in stage 3 of processing, a condition known as **associative agnosia**. Patients with agnosia thus appear to lack the neural machinery for forming particular kinds of internal representation.

Although Marr's theory was developed specifically for vision, its general strategy can be applied to all the sensory systems. At an abstract level they can all be considered as multi-stage information processing systems. Each stage computes an internal representation of some aspect of its sensory world, and passes that representation on to the next stage of processing.

Representation in perception

Marr's influential approach emphasized the importance of internal representations and computations in perception, so it is worth spending some time considering what these concepts mean in more detail. The concept of representation is quite general. You use representations all the time in everyday life; watches and clocks represent time, thermometers represent temperature, speedometers represent speed, maps represent spatial layout. Representations are powerful because they capture some aspect of reality and allow it to be manipulated and communicated. You can keep below the speed limit using a speedometer, or measure the distance between two towns using a map. In general a representation can be defined as a structure or state in one physical system that indicates a specific state or structure in another system. So the position of the needle in a speedometer

Key Terms

Apperceptive agnosia. A clinical visual disorder involving an inability to name, copy, or match even simple shapes.

Associative agnosia. A clinical visual disorder in which objects cannot be recognized from their shapes, even though they can be copied and matched with little difficulty.

indicates vehicle speed, and the height of mercury in a thermometer corresponds to ambient temperature.

In the context of perception, representational states must correspond to brain states and, as you know from earlier chapters, brain states correspond to particular patterns of neural activity evoked by sensory stimulation. So specific patterns of neural activity actually represent specific states in the outside world. When you see a tree, hear a bird, or feel a cold surface, you are activating internal representations of that particular sensory object and its properties; perceptions are representations in action. The idea that the whole of your perceived world is actually a representation of the outside world hidden away in your head can be quite hard to grasp initially. You perceive the world to be 'out there' but it is really tucked away between your ears.

Key Terms

Analog representation. A representational system in which continuously variable magnitudes in one physical system signify corresponding magnitudes in another system.

Symbolic representation. A representational system in which abstract, discrete symbols in one physical system signify discrete entities or states in another system.

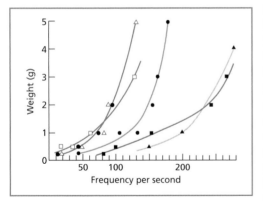

Figure 5.4 The relation between stimulus weight and response frequency for several afferent sensory nerves in a frog's muscle, shown by different symbols. Reproduced from Adrian and Zotterman (1926), with permission from Wiley-Blackwell.

Representations actually come in two forms, called **analog** and **symbolic**. In an analog representation, magnitudes in one physical system map onto analogous magnitudes in another system. So height in a mercury thermometer represents temperature; hand movement in a watch represents the passage of time; coordinates on a map represent location in space. In order to interpret an analog representation, you simply need to know the mapping rule that specifies the correspondence between the two systems (e.g. 'height represents temperature'). Analog representations are thought to be ubiquitous in sensory systems. One of the earliest lines of evidence came from research on frog sensory physiology. As Figure 5.4 illustrates, the rate of firing of afferent sensory nerves in a frog's muscle depends on mechanical load (muscle stretch). As more weight is applied to the muscle, so the rate of firing in the fiber increases (Adrian & Zotterman, 1926). Firing rate seems to represent load in an analog fashion. Notice that the relation between load and firing rate is not linear, but compressive in a way that is reminiscent of Fechner's Law (p. 57). Rate codes are used for many perceptual dimensions, such as loudness, head acceleration, mechanical pressure, and brightness contrast.

In a symbolic representation abstract, arbitrary symbols in one system correspond to entities or states in the other system. Symbolic representations in everyday usage tend to be based on numbers and letters. The numbers displayed on a digital thermometer (or clock) represent temperature (or time). In order to interpret a symbolic representation you need to know the lexicon of entries that map each symbol in one system onto a corresponding state in the other system. Think of the various labels used in different languages to represent temperature. In order to correctly select the hot tap (faucet) for washing your hands and the cold tap for brushing your teeth, you must make the correct connection between each symbol and a corresponding physical property (e.g. to brush your teeth in the UK you would select the tap labeled 'C', but this would be a mistake in France).

Symbolic representation lies at the heart of the *neuron doctrine of perception* (Barlow, 1972), which proposes that single neurons (or small groups of neurons) each code perceptually significant events and objects, such as your grandmother. The same cells would fire whenever your grandmother came into view. As you will see in the next chapter, there is some evidence that appears to support this idea.

Figure 5.5 contains a general functional diagram of perceptual processing, which makes the role of representation explicit. Each box corresponds to a separate stage of processing, and arrows represent the flow of information between one stage and another. Each stage can be identified with a specific population of neurons in the nervous system. As you saw in previous chapters, the different senses generally conform to this kind of processing scheme. After one or more synapses in the sense organ, signals travel along afferent fibers toward the thalamus. Neurons in the

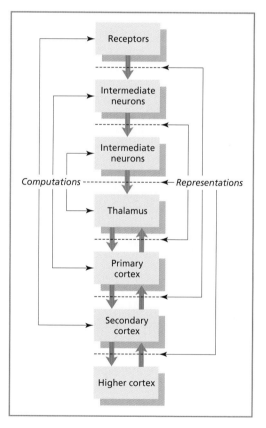

Figure 5.5 Representation and computation during hierarchical sensory processing. Each box corresponds to a population of neurons that receive an input representation from the previous stage of processing and compute an output representation for transmission to the next stage of processing.

thalamus then send the signals to primary sensory cortex, from where they travel on to secondary cortical areas. Information also flows down from the cortex to the thalamus. The information that is passed from one stage to the next contains a representation of some aspect of the outside world. Responses in gustatory fibers, for example, carry information that represents the sugar, salt, acid, plant alkaloid, and amino acid content of the substance currently sitting on the tongue. So any one stage of processing, any box in the diagram, receives a representation as input and produces a representation as an output. What happens inside each box?

Computation in perception

Each box in Figure 5.5 must transform its input in some way to create an output representation. This transformation is accomplished by the neurons that implement that stage of processing. You can describe the operation physiologically in terms of interactions between neurons, inhibition, excitation, and so on, or in more abstract mathematical terms. A good example is offered by neurons with center–surround receptive fields described in Chapter 2 (p. 30) and illustrated in Figures 2.3 and 2.7. They receive a pattern of activity from a group of receptors, either mechanoreceptors in the skin (Figure 2.3) that respond to mechanical distortion, or photoreceptors in the retina (Figure 2.7) that respond to light. The transform performed by the cell can be described in neural terms as follows. Some receptors excite the cell and others inhibit it, so the net response of the cell reflects a balance between excitation and inhibition. The anatomical structures involved in creating this pattern of excitation and inhibition are markedly different. In the case of photoreceptors, the neural circuit resides in the retina; in the case of mechanoreceptors the neural circuit resides in the brain stem. The transform performed by both kinds of center–surround cell can also be described in more abstract terms as follows. The neuron performs a simple mathematical computation; it calculates the difference in activation between the center of the receptive field and the surround. In mathematical terms the two receptive fields perform exactly the same computation. This goes back to Marr's distinction between neural implementations and computations. The same computation can be implemented by different neural structures.

Marr would ask: What is the goal of the computation performed by center–surround receptive fields? The answer to this question should reveal why two completely different neural circuits appear to be doing the same thing, computationally speaking. One overarching task of the perceptual systems is to tell us 'what is where', to paraphrase Marr. To do this they need to pick out objects against their background; they need to find the edges of objects. Visually, edges usually correspond to sudden changes in lightness at particular places in the image (e.g. the border between the light paper of a book and the dark fabric of a table-cloth). In the sense of touch, object borders usually correspond to sudden changes in textural properties (e.g. the smooth surface of paper and the rough surface of fabric). As you saw in Figures 2.3 and 2.7, center–surround receptive fields respond to spatial change much more than they do to uniform illumination or texture – they are change detec-tors designed to find the edges that usually mark the borders of objects. Recall a central tenet of information theory: efficient systems discard redundant information. Edges carry a great deal of information about object shape, but areas of even illumination or texture are relatively uninformative or redundant in this respect. Center–surround receptive fields preserve the most useful information and discard the redundant.

The general point to take from the example of the center–surround receptive field is that each of the transformations from input to output depicted in Figure 5.5 can be described in abstract terms as a compu-tational operation that transforms one representation into another. The notion of computation is very general, and is not restricted to arithmetic operations such as addition and subtraction, which can be applied to analog representations. Computations can also be performed on symbolic representations. In this case they typically involve true/false comparisons and equals assignments. An example of a simple symbolic computation would be:

IF <OBJECT SOUND=QUACK> **AND** <OBJECT LOCATION=WATER>
    THEN <OBJECT=DUCK>

In fact any manipulation of quantities or symbols according to a set of rules can be described as a computation. A specific set of rules to perform a particular computation is sometimes called an algorithm. Take the spell-checker in your word processor, email program or text message editor. It works by finding each string of letters enclosed by spaces, and comparing it against a stored list of known words. If a match is found, the word is deemed okay, but if no match is found the word is flagged as a spelling mistake. The spell-checking function is a computational process. It manipulates and compares representations of word strings according to a set of matching rules to produce an output (correct/incorrect). The same algorithm is implemented on many different hardware and software platforms, including various

PCs and phones. A more complicated version of this kind of computational process must take place in your head when you decide whether a word you are reading is spelled correctly, and even when you decide whether you recognize the person whose face you are looking at. The computation is more complex because you first have to extract and identify each letter (which can be quite difficult in handwriting), or extract the visual details in a face, before you can begin to compare the word or face against representations stored in your memory. Despite the complications, these mental computations are largely hidden and apparently effortless and rapid. The challenge of exposing and describing mental computations is one of the continuing fascinations of research in perception.

Evaluation

Internal representations are a central theme of this chapter. However, some theories of perception reject the notion of representation entirely. Connectionist theories model perception and cognition using large networks of simple but densely interconnected processing units (see Gurney, 2007). Activation arriving at input units spreads across the network until it arrives at an array of output units. No symbolic representations are computed, and there are no explicit rules; the network 'learns' how to produce an output from a given input. Connectionist theories do contain representations, but they are distributed among a large mass of units, rather than located in a relatively small number of units either as a quantity or a symbol. Recent discoveries of neurons with highly specific stimulus preferences (described in the next chapter) offer a severe challenge to connectionist theories, but do not rule them out completely (Plaut & McClelland, 2010). An influential early theory of perception known as 'direct' or 'ecological' perception (Gibson, 1950) emphasized the richness of the information available in natural stimuli, and also rejected the need for internal representations in the brain. This approach drastically underestimated the difficulty of picking up this information from natural stimuli.

Most modern theories of perception embrace the need for internal representations. They are built on mathematical foundations laid by Alan Turing, Claude Shannon, and David Marr. Nowadays all the perceptual systems are considered as information processing systems, and their properties are often characterized using functional block diagrams. Theories about specific functions

Key Term

Connectionist. A theoretical approach in computational neuroscience based on large networks of interconnected simple processing units.

Do I have pictures in my head?

Anatomy reveals that the eye forms an image very much like that inside a camera (Figure 1.7). Physiological data show that the visual cortex contains a topographical map of the visual field, albeit grossly distorted (Figure 3.4). Furthermore the notion that the brain creates internal representations of the world is central to modern theoretical approaches to perception. All of this might lead one to think that there is an 'inner screen' of some kind in the head, rather like a movie screen, and this internal image mediates conscious awareness (Frisby & Stone, 2010).

This *inner screen theory* certainly qualifies as a representational theory, because it does involve a representation, but it implies a very specific kind of representation. Each neuron in the screen describes the brightness of one particular spot in the world, rather like the pixels in a digital camera image: the more active the cell, the brighter the point in the world. However this is not how cortical cells work. Their responses are far more specific, as you saw in Chapter 3. Cortical cell response depends not on brightness, but on line orientation, motion direction, bright–dark contrast, colour, and so on. Different cells have different stimulus preferences.

However, there is a deeper problem with the inner screen theory. The inner screen only represents the properties of individual *points* in the visual scene, but recognition is based on *objects* in the scene and their properties. For example, you normally have little difficulty in recognizing chairs despite their huge variety of designs that manifest themselves as different images. Just from looking at a chair you can form a judgment as to whether it is too big or too small to sit on, whether it will be hard or soft, heavy or light. The inner screen theory has nothing to say about how or where these relatively abstract, symbolic object representations are created in the brain. Perceptual processing must move away from analog screen-like representations to more abstract, symbolic and semantic representations.

Many studies demonstrate that our internal representation of visual scenes has little in common with a photographic image. We retain only very sketchy details of the visual world from one glance to the next. For example, Tatler *et al.* (2003) briefly presented photographic images of real-world scenes to participants, and then asked them a series of questions about the content of the scenes. Responses indicated that participants retained only a relatively abstract representation of the gist of the scene and its general spatial layout, not a pictorial representation. 'Gist' refers to the general meaning or nature of a scene, such as whether it is a scene of an office or a kitchen.

can be developed and specified using mathematical tools such as information theory, and tested by implementing them on a computer. So mathematics underpins scientific psychology just as much as it underpins the traditional sciences of physics and chemistry.

Many of the detailed proposals Marr made about visual processing have not stood the test of time well (ironically his neural-based theory of the cerebellum has arguably fared better in this respect). For instance, Marr saw the flow of information as mostly in one direction only, from lower levels to higher, but downward information flow (**top-down processing**) is now thought to be crucial and highly significant theoretically, as you will see in Chapter 7. The downward flow of information to the thalamus is actually far greater than the upward flow. A second weakness in Marr's overall approach concerns one of his most influential ideas, the use of constraints to resolve ambiguity. Despite their power, in the very last paragraph of *Vision* he admitted that he had no general recipe for how they are discovered and assimilated into theory. A general mathematical framework within which to consider assumptions and constraints is now emerging which, as it happens, also addresses Marr's underestimation of top-down processing. Bayesian theories of perception seem to offer a promising way forward, and are described in Chapter 7.

Despite a lack of support for some of the details of Marr's theory, his general strategy for building theories has become ingrained in modern cognitive psychology and sensory neuroscience. In fact one could argue that Marr singlehandedly defined a new field of research, now called **computational neuroscience**. The great majority of researchers believe that perception does involve the creation of internal representations, and that mental processes are the methods used by the brain to compute those representations.

There is still some debate regarding the exact nature of internal representation in the brain. Marr argued that sensory representations are symbolic even at the very earliest stages of processing. More recent theories use analog representations much more extensively, as you will see in the next two chapters.

Key Terms

Top-down processing. A processing scheme in which information flows down from higher levels to lower levels of analysis, using prior knowledge and experience to steer lower level processes.

Computational neuroscience. A modern discipline that attempts to understand brain function by analyzing and simulating the computations that it performs.

Summary

- Modern theories of perception are based on conceptual foundations laid by three mathematicians; Alan Turing, Claude Shannon, and David Marr.
  - Turing established the mathematical basis for computer models of human perception and cognition.
  - Shannon's information theory supplies the mathematical tools for understanding information transmission in sensory systems.
  - Marr's theory of vision emphasized the need to consider perception at an abstract, computational level.
- Nearly all modern theories of perception are representational theories.
  - Internal representations correspond to particular patterns of brain activity, and can take two forms, analog and symbolic.
  - Each stage of sensory processing receives a representation from the previous stage, and passes on a new representation to the next stage.
  - The transformation from one representation into another can be described as a computation; manipulation of quantities and symbols based on a set of rules.

REFLECTIVE EXERCISE

1. Which of the following factors does not have a bearing on coding efficiency, according to information theory:
   a. Channel capacity
   b. Redundancy
   c. Noise
   d. Gist

2. Apply the concepts of representation and computation to what you know about neural processing in the olfactory system.

3. Evaluate how information theory can help us to understand the effectiveness of line drawings as visual representations.

FURTHER READING

- Farah, M.J. (2004) *Visual Agnosia*. Second Edition. Cambridge, MA: MIT Press.
- Frisby, J.P., & Stone, J.V. (2010) *Seeing: The Computational Approach to Biological Vision*. Cambridge, MA: MIT Press.
- Glennerster, A. (2007) Marr's vision: twenty-five years on. *Current Biology*, *17*, R397–R399.
- Quinlan, P., & Dyson, B. (2008) *Cognitive Psychology*. Harlow, UK: Pearson Education Ltd.
- Tatler, B.W. (2002) What information survives saccades in the real world? *Progress in Brain Research*, *140*, 149–163.

Population codes in perception   6

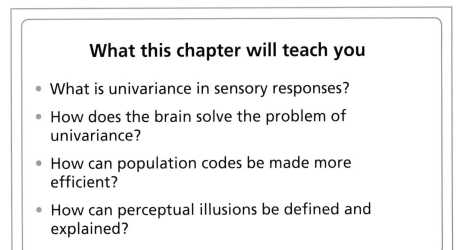

What this chapter will teach you

- What is univariance in sensory responses?
- How does the brain solve the problem of univariance?
- How can population codes be made more efficient?
- How can perceptual illusions be defined and explained?

Introduction

Having surveyed sensation from the perspectives of physiology, neuro-psychology, psychophysics, and computational theory you are now in a position to consider how to put them together to build theories of sensory coding and perception. Multi-stage processing is a common theme across all the perspectives. As you saw in the last chapter (see Figure 5.5) each stage of processing builds a representation of certain aspects of the world. Lower level stages compute relatively simple sensory

Key Term

Univariance. A computational problem in sensory coding arising from the fact that the response of a sensory neuron usually depends on several stimulus dimensions, but can only vary along one dimension.

attributes such as local contour orientation, sound source direction, or chemical composition. Higher level stages use this relatively primitive information to construct perceptual representations of object properties. In this chapter you will read about some specific issues that confront lower level processes when they try to compute simple attributes. The next chapter considers higher level computations.

As Cajal first recognized, the elementary building block in all theories of sensation and perception is the neuron. A fundamental computational problem arises as soon as one begins to think about how to use neural activity to encode sensory attributes, which arises from the 'Principle of **Univariance**'.

The principle of univariance

The principle was first identified by Naka and Rushton (1966) as a fundamental computational issue in color vision physiology. Each photoreceptor produces a graded change in electrical potential when struck by light. Its output depends on both the intensity of the incident light and its wavelength:

> But since output is of only one kind (univariant) it cannot give simultaneously separate information as to both intensity and wavelength.
>
> (Naka & Rushton, 1966, p. 538)

The left-hand graph of Figure 6.1 shows the electrical response of an individual cone photoreceptor as a function of the intensity of the light falling on it, for two different wavelengths (from Schneeweis & Schnapf, 1999). The filled circles represent response using a wavelength that is close to the receptor's peak response, at 500 nm. Response increases progressively as light intensity rises. The open symbols represent response to another wavelength, 660 nm. Again response increases with intensity, but at any one intensity the response to 660 nm is lower than the response to 500 nm. The difference in response is a reflection of the fact that all photoreceptors respond better to some wavelengths than to others (see Figure 1.9). Consider a specific response level in the photoreceptor, picked out by the dashed horizontal line drawn through the graph. The intersections of this activity level with the two response curves show that it could be

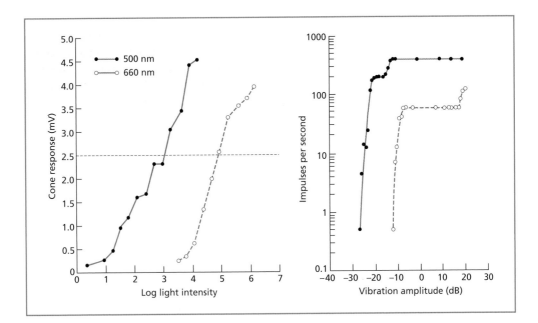

Figure 6.1 Univariance in sensory receptors. Left: Peak response of a red cone plotted as a function of light intensity for wavelengths of 500 nm (filled circles) and 660 nm (open circles). Adapted from Schneeweis and Schnapf (1999). Right: Firing rate in a Pacinian corpuscle as a function of vibration amplitude, at two vibration frequencies (open symbols: 60 Hz; filled symbols: 400 Hz). Adapted from Bolanowski and Zwislocki (1984).

produced by light of optimal wavelength but moderate intensity, or by a light of suboptimal wavelength but high intensity. The response is therefore ambiguous, and it cannot be used directly to code either intensity or wavelength.

Although the principle of univariance was first described in the context of color vision, it applies uniformly throughout the sensory systems. For instance, the right-hand graph in Figure 6.1 shows the electrical response of a skin mechanoreceptor (**Pacinian corpuscle**, as illustrated in Figure 1.2) as a function of the intensity of a mechanical stimulus (vibration amplitude), for different vibration frequencies (from Bolanoswski & Zwislocki, 1984). The dashed line across the graph shows that different combinations of vibration frequency and intensity can all produce the same response. One cannot infer both intensity and frequency from this individual cell's response. The problem is not restricted to receptor outputs, but applies

Key Term

Pacinian corpuscle. A type of sensory receptor that is sensitive to mechanical distortion; see Figure 1.2.

at all processing levels. The response of an individual cortical cell such as those shown in Figure 3.3 may depend on three or four stimulus dimensions (contrast, bar orientation, bar width, motion direction), yet can vary along only one dimension.

So a coding theory is required in order to explain how the character of a stimulus can be inferred from neural activity that is constrained by univariance. The general strategy adopted in theories of sensory coding is to combine the responses of different neurons together to create a **population code**.

Population codes

All sensory neurons respond quite selectively to incoming stimuli. Only certain stimuli are capable of driving the response of a particular cell, and different cells prefer different stimuli. So an entire stimulus dimension is encoded by a large array of neural units. Two examples can be seen in Figure 6.2, which shows cells in visual cortex tuned to grating spatial frequency or bar width (from De Valois et al., 1982) and cells in the auditory thalamus tuned to inter-aural delay (from Fitzpatrick et al., 1997). Each curve represents the response tuning of an individual cell. Only a small range of cells will respond to any given stimulus (a particular value on the x-axis), with cells tuned to that stimulus value responding most strongly. For example, Figure 6.3 shows the response of an array of orientation-tuned cells to an oriented visual stimulus. Notice that the responses do not lie on a perfectly smooth distribution of activity. They exhibit some degree of variability caused by moment-to-moment fluctuations in responsiveness (usually called neural 'noise'). The orientation of the stimulus can be computed by taking some statistical measure of the distribution, such as a weighted average of the responses. The averaging process serves to smooth out the noise in individual responses.

Population codes of this kind are very common in the nervous system, and are used in tasks such as memory and motor movement planning as well as in sensory processing (see, for example, Pouget et al., 2000). Their ability to accommodate noise by integrating information across many cells makes them an attractive computational solution to encoding simple stimulus attributes. They are also robust in the sense that damage or dysfunction in any one cell does not affect the overall computation performed by the population.

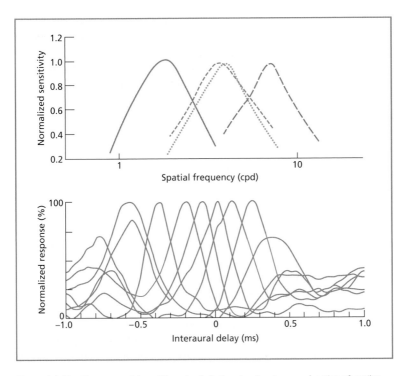

Figure 6.2 Top: Response of four different cells in the visual cortex as a function of grating spatial frequency. Bottom: Response of a number of cells in the auditory thalamus as a function of inter-aural delay.

Trichromacy

Light wavelength coding offers a good example of how a very simple population code can be used to encode values along a stimulus dimension. An ability to distinguish light wavelength is particularly useful when searching for food. Fruit and leaves can be picked out against a background of dappled shade. Ripe fruit can be discriminated from unripe fruit by virtue of the fact that it reflects more light in the longer wavelength region of the visible spectrum (its looks red rather than green). How can the human visual system disentangle

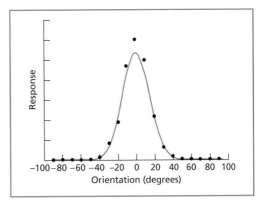

Figure 6.3 Hypothetical response in a population of orientation-selective cortical cells in the presence of a vertically oriented pattern. From Fitzpatrick *et al.* (1997). Reprinted by permission from Macmillan Publishers Ltd.

wavelength information from intensity, and solve the problem posed by univariance?

Figure 1.9 showed that there are three classes of cone photoreceptor, conventionally labeled as blue, green, and red cone types according to the wavelengths they can detect (though green and red cones overlap considerably in their sensitivity). Light at any one wavelength produces three numbers, corresponding to the activation levels of the three cone classes. Each wavelength is associated with a unique combination of cone outputs, offering a method of coding wavelength in terms of the pattern of responses across the cones. For example, a light from the short-wavelength region of the spectrum around 425 nm produces a much greater response in 'blue' cones than in either 'red' or 'green' cones. On the other hand a long-wavelength light above about 570 nm produces a large response in 'red' cones and virtually no response in 'blue' cones. The theory that wavelength is encoded by the relative activity across the three cone types is called trichromacy theory.

Most light sources emit energy at a broad range of visible wavelengths, and natural surfaces reflect a broad range of incident wavelengths, but the relative intensity at different reflected wavelengths depends on the properties of the surface. Grass, for example, reflects a high proportion of incident light at middle wavelengths around 550 nm, while tomatoes reflect predominantly in the region above 600 nm (this intrinsic physical property of an object is called its spectral reflectance). However, no matter how many wavelengths are present in the light reflected from a surface, the cones only ever produce three numbers corresponding to the responses of the three cone classes, so there is some scope for confusion (Lennie, 2000). Trichromacy theory makes a strong prediction: Two surfaces that reflect completely different sets of wavelengths will nevertheless be indistinguishable to a human observer with normal color vision – they will appear the same hue – if they produce the same relative responses across the three cone classes. Such surfaces or lights do actually exist, and are called metamers.

The hypothetical example in Figure 6.4 shows how trichromacy can explain the apparent equality of metameric colors. It shows triplets of cone responses to each of

Key Terms

Trichromacy theory. The theory that color appearance can be explained by the pattern of responses across the three types of cone receptor in the human retina.

Spectral reflectance. The proportion of incident light reflected from a surface at different wavelengths in the spectrum.

Hue. Sensory impression of the color of a light or a surface, such as 'red', 'magenta', or 'green'.

Metamer. Two colors or lights that appear the same hue but contain different light wavelengths.

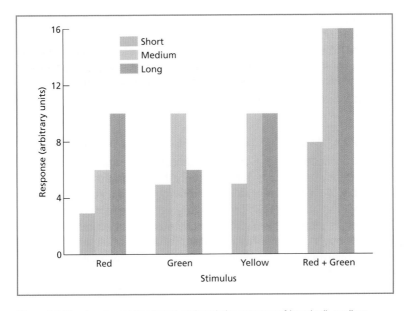

Figure 6.4 Wavelength encoding based on the relative response of long (red), medium (green) and short (blue) cone classes. Each bar shows the activity in red, green and blue cone types in response to the relevant wavelength or mixture of wavelengths.

four colored lights. The red light on the far left produces the strongest response in red cones, while the green light (middle left) excites green cones the most. A yellow light (middle right) produces equal responses in red and green cones. So one can perceive that the red, green, and yellow lights are different on the basis of the different pattern of responses they create across the cone types. The bars on the far right show the triplet of cone responses to a light that contains a mixture of red and green wavelengths. The response of each cone type corresponds to the sum of its responses to the red and green lights when presented separately (add up the corresponding bars on the middle and far left to produce the bars on the far right). Notice that the relative response across the cone types to the red/green mixture is identical to the relative response to the pure yellow light. So the red/green mixture is perceptually indistinguishable from yellow; the two lights are metamers.

Psychophysical studies of human color matching produce results that are consistent with trichromacy theory, and can be predicted quite closely by the relative sensitivities of red, green, and blue cones (Baylor, 1987). In fact one never needs more than three different wavelengths in order to produce a subjective match with *any* visible color. This basic principle of color vision is exploited in television and computer displays. Each picture element or pixel on the screen is made up of three dots, emitting in the red, green, and blue parts of the spectrum. A wide gamut of colors can be produced on the screen by altering the relative intensities of the three dots.

Sparse codes and inhibition

Population codes have a major weakness: they are quite wasteful, because they necessarily involve activity that is spread among a large ensemble of cells. Recent studies of energy demand in the brain have revealed that, in metabolic terms, it is a very expensive organ to run. The brain is small (typically 5% of body mass), but accounts for 20% of the body's overall energy consumption in adult humans (the consumption of energy by the brain remains constant regardless of the level of mental activity, so you cannot think yourself thin). Electrical activity in cortical neurons obviously requires energy, so it is not surprising that the huge mass of cells in the cerebral cortices consumes 44% of the brain's energy supply (Lennie, 2003). The brain simply cannot afford high levels of activity in large ensembles of neurons; one estimate suggests that only 10% or less of cortical cells can be active at any one time. So how can the brain afford to use population codes so widely?

The answer to this question is that the brain takes steps to maximize coding efficiency, conveying the maximum amount of information with the minimum level of neural activity; a **sparse code** in which many of the neurons in a population are silent, and a given percept is represented by activity in a very small ensemble of active neurons. As you saw in the previous chapter, one way to improve coding efficiency is to reduce redundancy in the signal by removing response components that do not convey useful information. So what can be done to reduce redundancy in population codes and so make them more sparse? Natural sensory stimuli are in fact highly redundant. For example, if an oriented contour is found at a particular location in a natural image, it is highly likely that similarly oriented contours will be found nearby. A moment's reflection will bring to mind many examples: blades of grass in a meadow or hairs on a person's head that all tend to point in the same direction. The same applies to other features such as

Key Term

Sparse code. An efficient form of population coding characterized by strong activity in only a small subset of the neural population; it can be achieved using inhibitory interactions between the neurons.

shape, size, color, and depth; for instance, the shape, size, and color of a pebble on a beach tend to be very similar to pebbles lying nearby. Stimuli are also highly correlated over time, because object properties tend to persist over time. Moving objects (and all the features lying on them) tend to continue to move; sounds such as wind noise tend to persist at least for a short time. The neural responses evoked by natural stimuli necessarily show the same kinds of spatial and temporal redundancy as the stimuli themselves. So cells tuned to nearby locations on a sensory dimension tend to have similar response levels, which often change over time only gradually. Such redundant activity can be reduced using inhibition that spreads over space and over time. You have seen such inhibitory processes in action in previous chapters. The lateral inhibition built into center–surround receptive fields in vision and in somatosensation (see pp. 26 and 30) reduces spatial redundancy. Adaptation effects serve to reduce temporal redundancy (see Wark *et al.*, 2007).

Sparseness in coding requires that cell responses are attenuated or inhibited selectively, to preserve differences in neural response while discarding similar responses. So cells tuned to similar stimuli should inhibit each other. The inhibition can come either from lateral connections between cells in the same population, or via 'vertical' connections from cell populations at other levels in the processing hierarchy. Both forms of inhibition have been found in the brain.

The sparsest possible code would be activity in a single cell at the pinnacle of the processing hierarchy that encodes a complex, abstract entity such as personal identity (the grandmother cells mentioned in earlier chapters; Barlow, 1972). Some recent research appears at first glance to be consistent with this extreme form of sparse coding. One experiment recorded activity from individual cells in the human medial temporal lobe (MTL) during procedures to treat epilepsy (electrodes were implanted in MTL to locate the focus of seizures). About 40% of the cells studied were very highly selective in their responses. Some cells responded vigorously to various images of the actress Jennifer Aniston, for example, but were silent in the presence of all other images tested. Although these cells bear some similarities to what one would expect to see in archetypal grandmother cells, the research team that found them backed away from such an interpretation (Quiroga *et al.*, 2007). It is extremely unlikely, they argue, that just one or two cells from the hundreds of millions in MTL code for Jennifer Aniston, and that these cells just happen to have been found in a study employing pictures of her. Moreover, one cannot be absolutely certain that the cells are in fact uniquely selective to Jennifer Aniston, because only a relatively small number of images could be presented during a recording session lasting approximately 30 minutes. So Quiroga *et al.* (2007) argue that their research is consistent with a sparse coding strategy in this high-level cortical area associated with visual memory: On the basis of statistical calculations they estimate that fewer than two million of the approximately one billion cells in the MTL might represent a given percept (1 in 500,000 cells).

Illusions

Sparse coding and illusions

Perceptual illusions offer a glimpse of the computations that underlie perceptual judgments, and can often be explained using sparse codes. Targeted inhibition in the orientation domain serves to reduce redundancy in the output of orientation-tuned neurons: cells tuned to one orientation at a particular image location inhibit the activity of cells tuned to similar orientations at nearby locations. However a side-effect of this redundancy reduction is to produce slight distortions in population response that emphasize change in orientation at nearby locations. A demonstration is depicted in Figure 6.5. It shows the population of orientation-tuned cells depicted in Figure 6.3, responding to a pattern oriented at zero degrees (vertical). Inhibition caused by a surrounding pattern (purple line and diamonds) peaks at a slightly clockwise angle of +10 degrees. Net response (blue line and open circles) is calculated by summing the excitation (purple line) with the inhibition (green line). It shows a reduction in overall population response of some 30% (compare the areas under the curves), so the inhibition succeeds in promoting coding sparseness. However it also alters the shape of the activity profile. The population response peaks at a slightly anti-clockwise angle of −5 degrees. The consequence for perception should be an exaggeration of the angular difference between nearby lines at different orientations. A number of well-known geometrical illusions show such an exaggeration in apparent angle, as illustrated

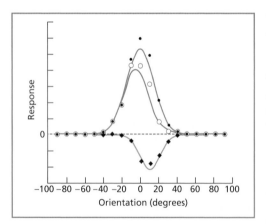

Figure 6.5 Effect of inhibition on the hypothetical population response in orientation-selective cells. Excitation (purple line) peaks at 0 degrees, and inhibition (green line) peaks at +10 degrees, so the net response (blue line) peaks at −5 degrees.

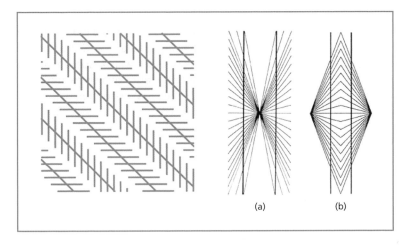

Figure 6.6 Three geometrical visual illusions that involve distortion produced by the apparent expansion of acute angles (the Zollner, Hering, and Wundt illusions, reading from left to right).

in Figure 6.6, and it is very likely that this angle expansion is caused by inhibition (Blakemore et al., 1970; Tolhurst & Thompson, 1975).

Most people view perceptual illusions as curiosities; captivating, counterintuitive demonstrations of the fallibility of the perceptual systems. They are considered to be errors or mistakes in which perceptions do not agree with reality. Illusions are reported frequently during interactions with modern media reconstructions of reality. For example, when you listen to music on headphones, you may perceive sounds that appear to emanate from a particular direction in space, even though you know that there are no musicians sitting in front of you. When you watch a movie you may perceive realistic dynamic action, even though you know that the movie is really a series of static frames presented in rapid succession. If you are viewing a film projected in 3-D stereo, you may perceive objects floating in space in the middle of the theater.

What is an illusion?

Scientists are interested in illusions primarily because they shed light on the usually hidden computations that are used to extract meaningful information from the world. However, a careful scientific analysis would reveal that many perceptual effects should not really be considered as illusions at all. The usual definition of a perceptual illusion as an error or mistake that does not agree with reality (see Gregory, 1997) involves two implicit assumptions about perception and about reality. First, it assumes that the purpose of perception is to measure reality as accurately as possible. Second, it assumes that there is some independent, objective measure of reality that can be compared against perception. In many cases one or the other of these two assumptions does not hold, so the percept cannot be considered as an illusion.

Let's start with the first assumption that the purpose of perception is to measure reality as accurately as possible. Computational considerations discussed in the previous chapter would challenge this assumption. One could argue, as Marr and others have, that the purpose of perception is to tell us about important aspects of the world – what objects are present, where they are, what they might do next. Clearly these are more sophisticated tasks than 'measure accurately', and may entail computations that do not place a high premium on simple measurement accuracy. Take the humble center–surround receptive fields that you have encountered a number of times in previous chapters. Computational considerations indicate that they are designed to preserve information about change (because change signifies object boundaries) and discard uniformity (because it is redundant). A by-product of this design feature is that center–surround responses accentuate edges and corners. The pyramid illusion (Figure 6.7, left) contains a series of overlaid squares, each successive square is smaller and lighter than the last (see the enlargement in Figure 6.7, right). Bright rays are seen radiating from the center of the pattern, even though none are present in the image. The illusion arises directly from center–surround responses that serve to accentuate corners (see Morgan, 1996). The enlargement in Figure 6.7 (right) shows two receptive fields with an excitatory center, one positioned at a corner and one along a side (positioned at the same lightness level). The ring-shaped inhibitory surround receives less light overall at the corner (as indicated by the dark regions) than along the side, so cells positioned at the corners should be more active than those along the sides, resulting in the bright rays. The illusion is not a mistake as such, because it comes from a deliberate design feature – a particular way of measuring patterns using center–surround receptive fields.

Now let's turn to the assumption that certain percepts are illusions because they do not agree with objective measurement of reality. It begs the question: What is reality? Imagine that you have decided to replace the floor covering in your kitchen. So you arrange for several different companies to measure the room area and quote a

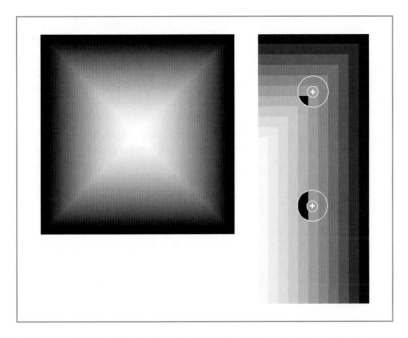

Figure 6.7 The pyramid illusion. Left: The image contains a series of overlaid rectangles, progressively decreasing in size and increasing in lightness. Right: Enlarged section, with superimposed center–surround receptive fields. Inhibition is weaker in the receptive field positioned at the corner.

price. Three different representatives measure the kitchen, using different techniques. One uses a retractable steel rule, another uses a laser ranging device, and a third uses a wooden meter rule. All are legitimate, 'objective' ways to make measurements, but when the quotes arrive you discover that the different measurements disagree. Do you assume that one measurement is correct and the others are incorrect? If so, how do you decide which is correct? If you decide that the measurement based on the laser ranging device is likely to be the most accurate, does that mean that the other measures are 'illusory'? Not really; they represent different but equally legitimate ways of taking the same measurement, though one cannot reasonably expect them to agree exactly. Different measurement methods may be subject to slightly different biases, or independent random errors. Even when the same measurement is repeated there are likely to be differences caused by small measurement errors. In the case of rules, for example, one must rely on the accuracy of the scale markings

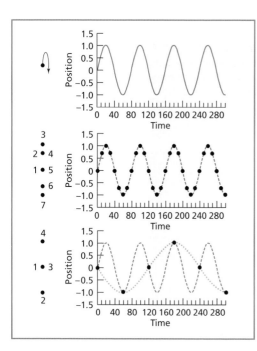

Figure 6.8 Apparent motion. Top: The graph plots the vertical position of a continuously oscillating dot as a function of time. The motion creates a smooth wave. Middle: The moving dot is represented by a series of snapshots taken at intervals of 10 time units (black dots). Its trajectory can be recovered by fitting a smooth curve to the discrete positions (dashed line). Bottom: When the snapshots are taken less frequently (intervals of 60 time units), the dot's trajectory cannot be recovered accurately using curve fitting (dotted line).

and the mechanical stability of the material (metal or wood), as well as the competence of the person reading the scale.

This line of argument can be applied directly to the sensory systems. To take an example mentioned earlier, there are several ways to compute a perceptual estimate of sound source location, including inter-aural time differences, inter-aural intensity differences, and visual cues. A measurement can be computed from one cue by specialized neurons in the absence of other cues, and can contribute to a perception of sound source location. That measurement cannot be considered illusory just because it occurs without measures from other cues, or even in the presence of a slightly different value from another measure. So in this sense the sound field you experience while wearing stereo headphones is not an illusion, but a legitimately derived measure of sound source location, as far as the auditory system is concerned.

RESEARCH QUESTION

Is the visual movement perceived in movie films an illusion?

Movie films contain a series of static frames presented in rapid succession, yet you see realistic dynamic scenes full of naturalistic movement. The movement you perceive in the movie is often described as an illusion, but this is arguably a misconception. Figure 6.8 illustrates why. The image at the top left represents a very simple moving display in which a single dot oscillates up and down repeatedly. The smooth curve in the graph on the right plots the vertical position of the dot over time. The continuous up-and-down motion creates a wave in the graph. One can take snapshots of the moving dot at regular time intervals. The image at the middle left shows seven successive dot positions ('frames'), based on snapshots taken every 10 time units. The dots in the middle graph show the position of the dot at each of these time intervals. The snapshots are sufficiently frequent to permit one to reconstruct the trajectory of the dot by fitting a smooth curve through the discrete samples, shown by the dashed line. Notice that the curve described by the dashed line matches very closely the original smooth trajectory of the dot shown in the upper graph, so it is possible to recover the motion of the dot accurately using only the snapshots.

The snapshots are equivalent to the individual frames that would be recorded by a cine camera trained on the moving dot. The brain could recover the trajectory of the dot from these samples using a computational process that is equivalent mathematically to curve-fitting. So the resulting impression of motion is not an illusion, but can be derived from physical information that is available in the movie, and computed by a neural process akin to curve-fitting. There is a good deal of physiological and psychophysical evidence that the brain really does implement a smooth curve-fitting procedure of this kind when you perceive motion (Morgan, 1980; Burr & Ross, 1986). What if the samples are taken less frequently, as shown at the bottom of Figure 6.8? Here the snapshots are taken at intervals of 60 time units, shown by the black dots. Now curve-fitting cannot accurately recover the trajectory of the dot, because there is too little information. In fact the best-fitting curve through the available dot positions corresponds to a dot that often moves in the opposite direction to the original stimulus, shown by the dotted curve in the bottom graph. Notice that from 'frame 1' to 'frame 2' in the lower left, the dot shifts in a downward direction, whereas the actual motion is upward. You see this kind of reversed motion when viewing rapidly rotating wheels in films, such as wagon wheels or car wheels. The 'wagon-wheel' effect, as it is often called, occurs when the movement captured in the film is too rapid given the rate at which snapshots are taken by the cine camera (Finlay et al., 1984). It is a moot point whether you should call the wagon-wheel effect an illusion. It is clearly erroneous, but it is a physical problem caused by sampling limitations. Any device, whether mechanical, electronic, or neural, would be prone to the error. A more accurate description of the effect would be that it is a 'sampling artifact'.

On the other hand, the motion seen in a stationary pattern following adaptation (the motion after-effect described in Chapter 4) can be confidently classified as an illusion because there is no physical information at all in the image that corresponds to it.

Evaluation

Population coding plays a crucial role in computational theories of coding in the central nervous system because it solves the problem of univariance in neural activity. Sparse codes can be achieved using targeted inhibition. The principle is so deeply ingrained in theories of sensation and perception that more often than not it is not made explicit in the description of a theory, but taken as a given. However it is important not to lose sight of the population codes lying within perceptual theories, and the rationale for their adoption.

Illusions represent one of the most misunderstood aspects of perception. Many phenomena are labeled as 'illusions' incorrectly, because of lack of understanding. Most researchers do not actually spend much time pondering whether a particular perceptual effect can or cannot justifiably be classified as an 'illusion'. Indeed the term is often used quite loosely as shorthand for any effect that clearly demonstrates the outcome of computational processing in the sensory systems, without implying that the effect is a mistake or error. As such they often inspire new lines of research inquiry. The challenge is to place explanations of illusions within a broader functional context in terms of the tasks performed by the sensory systems.

Summary

- Activity in sensory neurons is inherently ambiguous because it depends on several stimulus parameters in combination (univariance).
- The problem of univariance can be solved by comparing activity across an ensemble of neurons, a population code.
- Population codes can be made more energy efficient (sparse coding) using targeted inhibition that reduces responses in neurons carrying redundant information.
- Many perceptual illusions can be explained using theories based on population coding, but some phenomena are mislabeled as illusions because they are assumed to result from errors or inaccuracies in perceptual coding.

REFLECTIVE EXERCISE

1. An individual sensory neuron's response can vary only along one dimension, but it depends on several stimulus dimensions. This principle is called:
   a. Specific nerve energy
   b. Cortical magnification
   c. Univariance
   d. Population coding

2. Describe how you could explain your ability to distinguish the taste of tomato puree from the taste of raspberry puree using a population code.

3. Most color printers use only three colored inks (cyan, magenta, and yellow). Explain how this relates to the properties of human color vision.

FURTHER READING

- Clifford, C.W.G., Wenderoth, P., & Spehar, B. (2000) A functional angle on some after-effects in cortical vision. *Proceedings of the Royal Society of London, Series B, 267*, 1705–1710.
- Eagleman, D.M. (2001) Visual illusions and neurobiology. *Nature Reviews Neuroscience, 2*, 920–926.
- Lennie, P. (2000). Color vision: putting it all together. *Current Biology, 10*, R589–R591.
- Morgan, M.J. (1996) Visual illusions. In V. Bruce (ed.) *Unsolved Mysteries of the Mind* (pp. 29–58). Hove, UK: Lawrence Erlbaum Associates Ltd.
- Pouget, A., Dayan, P., & Zemel, R. (2000) Information processing with population codes. *Nature Reviews Neuroscience, 1*, 125–132.

Perceptual inference 7

What this chapter will teach you

- Why are sensory data ambiguous?

- How can sensory ambiguity be resolved?

- What experimental techniques can be used to study ambiguity resolution, and what do they reveal?

- How can Bayesian theories help to explain ambiguity resolution?

Introduction

Chapter 6 discussed how simple perceptual attributes such as line orientation, sound source direction, and tactile vibration frequency are encoded using **population codes** or **sparse codes**. These codes constitute initial measurements of the primitive sensory properties of objects. At the

Key Terms

Population code. A processing scheme in which different values of a stimulus attribute such as color or tilt are coded by different patterns of activity in a population of neurons.

Sparse code. An efficient form of population coding characterized by strong activity in only a small subset of the neural population; it can be achieved using inhibitory interactions between the neurons.

next level of processing these measurements must be combined to construct perceptual representations of larger structures and objects, as depicted for vision in the hierarchical scheme of Figure 5.3. The processes that combine initial descriptions into global structures or object descriptions face a familiar fundamental problem: ambiguity. This time the ambiguity does not come from univariance in neural codes, but from the inherent limitations of sensory information, and it poses a challenge for any system hoping to make sense of the data, whether a neural system (a brain) or an electronic one (a computer).

As an example, consider the problem facing the visual system, illustrated in Figure 7.1. In the middle is the stimulus for vision, the retinal image. The content of this image at any given instant is created by the interaction of many different factors, some of which are shown along the bottom and include the objects present, their layout, the position of the observer, the direction of the light source, and so on. A change in

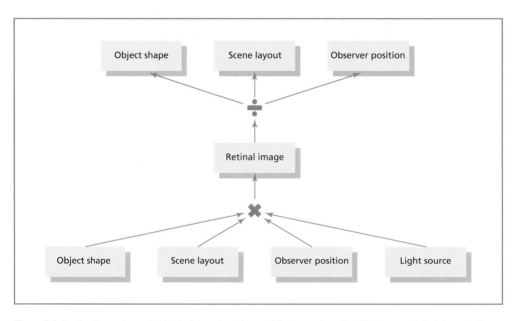

Figure 7.1 A retinal image is created by the interaction of several factors such as the objects present, their layout in the scene, the position of the observer, and the light source. The task of the visual system is to divide up or decompose the image into the contributions from these different factors.

any one element can have dramatic consequences over large areas of the image. In order to interpret the image correctly the visual system must recover the contribution that each factor makes to the pattern of light evident in the image, as shown at the top. This task is formidably difficult. It is comparable to the mathematical problem of factorization, in which a number is decomposed into other numbers that when multiplied together give the original number. Numbers that are not prime numbers may have many possible factorizations. The number 96, to take a random example, can be decomposed into (12×8) or (6×16) or (4×24) or ($2 \times 6 \times 8$) and so on. Without any supplementary information it is not possible, given only the outcome, to know what combination of numbers produced it. An exactly equivalent problem faces the sensory systems. Given a particular pattern of sensory data (a specific outcome) it is not possible to deduce the specific objects, layout, viewer position, and so on that created it, at least on the basis of the sensory data alone.

A specific visual example of this kind of ambiguity is shown in Figure 7.2. The image on the retina (shown at the bottom as a cast shadow) is inherently ambiguous, because there are an infinite number of object shapes that could all produce this image. Just three of them are shown above the image in Figure 7.2. Despite a common preference for perceiving this image as a cube, there is no information in the image itself to specify this interpretation over all the alternatives.

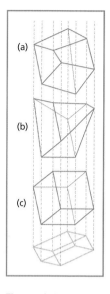

Figure 7.2 Ambiguity in projected images. The image at the bottom could potentially be created by an infinite variety of different objects; three possible objects are shown above the image. Reprinted from Ernst and Bulthoff (2004), copyright 2004, with permission from Elsevier.

Bottom-up and top-down processing in perception

As Marr recognized, the ambiguity illustrated in Figures 7.1 and 7.2 is unavoidable. How can it be resolved? More information is needed than is available in the sensory data, in the form of constraints or assumptions that allow the system to reject the great majority of the potential interpretations. In the case of the shape in Figure 7.2, visual processing could impose a solution using the assumption that natural object shapes tend to be balanced and symmetrical. There are two possible routes that the additional information can take during perceptual analysis, known as **bottom-up processing** and **top-down processing**.

In bottom-up processing, ambiguity is resolved as the signals travel 'up' the processing chain from lower levels, using constraints that are hard-wired into the

Key Terms

Bottom-up processing. A processing scheme in which information flows up from lower levels to higher levels of analysis, integrating simple sensory attributes into large structures on the basis of built-in rules.

Top-down processing. A processing scheme in which information flows down from higher levels to lower levels of analysis, using prior knowledge and experience to steer lower level processes.

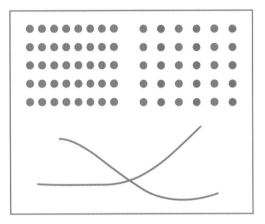

Key Term

Gestalt psychology. A theoretical movement that emphasized perceptual grouping on the basis of a set of rules or laws such as similarity and proximity.

Figure 7.3 Demonstrations of Gestalt grouping. The dots at top left are grouped into rows on the basis of proximity; the dots at top right are grouped into columns on the basis of similarity; the lines at the bottom form two curves, rather than two angles touching at their tips.

processing scheme. Gestalt grouping principles offer a good example of constraints built in to bottom-up processes. In the early twentieth century the **Gestalt psychologists** identified a set of rules or 'laws' of perceptual organization, which describe how the visual system appears to have some in-built preferences for grouping parts of the image together on the basis of certain simple sensory properties (Rock & Palmer, 1990). These properties include spatial proximity, similarity in color, similarity in size, and good continuation (smooth curves). Figure 7.3 shows some examples. Gestalt grouping laws constitute assumptions based on the properties of real-world objects and scenes, which help to resolve ambiguity. Objects tend to be cohesive, opaque, and made from relatively few materials. So nearby or similar elements in the image are likely to have come from the same real-world object and can be grouped together. Similarly, natural objects tend to have smooth shapes with relatively few sharp angles, so grouping can be biased to favor smooth changes in contour orientation. So certain assumptions about the nature of the sensory input may be built into the computations performed by bottom-up processes.

In top-down processing, signals travel back down the processing hierarchy so that information from high levels of processing is fed back to lower levels to steer their output. This information takes the form of prior knowledge or expectation about the nature of the sensory input. An example is shown in Figure 7.4. In the absence of other information, you may see nothing meaningful in it. But if you know that it shows a woman's face, a meaningful interpretation may become apparent. On the other hand, if you are told that it is a man playing a saxophone, a different interpretation may emerge.

All the empirical techniques that you have read about in previous chapters, such as psychophysics and neuroimaging, can be used to clarify the roles played by bottom-up and top-down processing. In the next section you will read about several stimulus paradigms that have

Figure 7.4 What do you see? From Mooney (1957).

been particularly informative in this regard. As you will see, there is actually evidence to support both theories. Bottom-up processes appear more important for some stimuli, and top-down processes appear more important for others. The chapter concludes with a detailed discussion of a particular theory of top-down inference in perception, called Bayesian inference.

The perception of ambiguous stimuli

Ambiguity resolution is a core function of higher level perceptual processing stages. In order to study the processes that resolve ambiguity, researchers often use stimuli that are carefully designed to create specific kinds of ambiguity. They assume that discoveries made using these degenerate stimuli will shed light on the normal processes of ambiguity resolution in the sensory systems. This is a fast-moving, dynamic research area in perception, driven by recent developments in empirical methodology (fMRI, described in Chapter 3) and in theoretical models (Bayesian inference, explained later).

Bistable stimuli

Figure 7.5 shows examples of several visual stimuli that admit two equally plausible interpretations. In the Necker cube (Figure 7.5a), the vertical face at the lower left can be seen as either at the front or at the back of the cube. In Figure 7.5b the line drawing can be seen as either

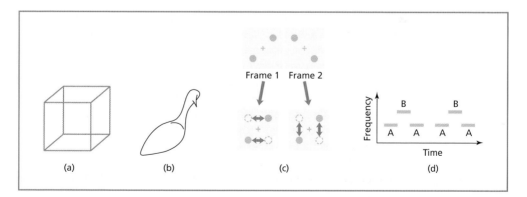

Figure 7.5 Bistable stimuli. (a) The face at the lower left of the cube can be seen as either at the front or at the back. (b) The line drawing can be interpreted as either a shoe or a bird. (Drawing by Jocelyn Cammack.) (c) The dots in this two-frame motion display can be seen either in horizontal motion or in vertical motion. (d) An alternating sequence of higher and lower pitch tones (A and B) can be heard either as a single galloping rhythm (A–B–A, A–B–A, . . .) or as two separate beats (A–A–A . . ., B–B–B . . .).

a shoe or a bird. Figure 7.5c is an ambiguous motion quartet; alternating presentation of pairs of dots in diagonally opposite corners of a virtual square results in bistable perception of horizontal and vertical motion; sometimes the dots appear to move horizontally, and at other times they appear to move vertically. Figure 7.5d shows an ABA auditory 'streaming' sequence. Tones of two frequencies, A and B, follow each other in a rapid repeating sequence. Listeners sometimes hear the sequence as a single galloping rhythm ('da di da – da di da – da di da – . . .'), and sometimes as two separate beating sequences ('da da da . . .' and 'di di di . . .').

What drives the alternation between the two percepts in each of these bistable stimuli; bottom-up or top-down processes? Bottom-up explanations argue that the two stimuli generate competing population codes in stimulus-selective neurons. Once one population response gains the upper hand it dominates perception, but neural adaptation weakens its grip and allows the alternate population response to take over. After a short time adaptation kicks in again to bring the first response back to dominance. Cycling adaptation in low-level population codes is thus a plausible explanation for the alternations found in bistable perception. In top-down explanations, on the other hand, bistable perception results from indecision on the part of high-level processes regarding the most plausible interpretation of the stimulus, perhaps driven by shifts in attention.

In the case of auditory streaming (Figure 7.5d), evidence indicates that bottom-up processing in the brain stem and cortex drives the alternation. Microelectrode recordings in monkeys, bats, and starlings show that adaptation in frequency-selective cortical neurons can explain many of the features of auditory streaming (Micheyl et al., 2007). However top-down processing does seem to drive another unstable auditory percept called verbal transformation, in which prolonged listening to a word that is repeated without a pause results in apparent transformations of the word sound. For example, when the word 'tress' is repeated ('tresstresstresstress . . .') it may be heard as cycling between 'dress', 'stress', 'drest', or even 'Esther'. When the word 'life' is repeated continuously ('lifelifelifelifelife . . .') perception alternates in a bistable fashion between 'life' and 'fly'. Kondo and Kashino (2007) used fMRI to study the brain areas associated with these transformations. They found that transitions between perceived words were linked to significant activation in areas of the frontal lobe (prefrontal cortex and anterior cingulate cortex) that are involved in

Key Term

Frontal lobe. One of the four lobes of the cerebral cortex, thought to be essential for planning and controlling behavior.

high-level speech processing. Kondo and Kashino (2007) suggested that these frontal areas may generate verbal forms that are fed back down to lower levels of auditory cortex to influence the transitions that are encoded.

Adaptation experiments using bistable visual stimuli also find evidence for the involvement of both bottom-up and top-down processes. Long and Moran (2007) studied the Necker cube (Figure 7.5a). They found that prior exposure to an unambiguous version of the figure biased subsequent perception of the ambiguous figure in favor of the alternate percept, consistent with bottom-up adaptation. Sterzer and Kleinschmidt (2007) used fMRI to study the ambiguous motion display shown in Figure 7.5c. When the two alternate paths (vertical and horizontal) are equal in length, perception repeatedly alternates between the directions given by the two paths in an apparently random fashion. However it is possible to impose a perceptual bias favoring one of the paths by making that path shorter than the alternate path. Sterzer and Kleinschmidt first presented the stimulus with equal path lengths, and recorded activation in several cortical areas while the participants reported the spontaneous alternations in apparent direction that they experienced. Then the researchers manipulated the path length in the stimulus so as to bias it in such a way that apparent direction switched at exactly the same times that participants had previously reported spontaneous switches in the ambiguous version of the display. Comparison of the brain activation patterns in ambiguous and unambiguous alternations allowed Sterzer and Kleinschmidt to identify the brain areas whose activation preceded spontaneous reversals, and therefore presumably drove the reversals. They found that activation in the frontal and **parietal lobes** preceded spontaneous perceptual reversals. These areas are known to be involved in attention, and so implicate a top-down explanation for the motion ambiguity.

There has been relatively little research to date on bistable perception in touch. Carter *et al.* (2008) used a tactile version of the bistable motion display depicted in Figure 7.5c. The stimulus was created by 200 ms bursts of vibrotactile stimulation applied to the finger pads in a spatial configuration corresponding to the quartet display. Subjects perceived tactile motion traveling across the fingertip that alternated between the two possible directions (as depicted in Figure 7.5c). Adaptation to a quartet that was biased to favor one of the directions caused subsequent perception of the

Key Term

Parietal lobe. One of the four lobes of the cerebral cortex, thought to be important for guiding selective attention to stimuli.

ambiguous stimulus to be biased in favor of the other direction. The fact that adaptation can alter the perceived direction of the ambiguous tactile stimulus favors a bottom-up account of tactile alternation.

Rivalrous stimuli

So-called 'rivalrous' stimuli offer another experimental paradigm for studying perceptual ambiguity. In a rivalrous stimulus two unrelated stimuli are presented simultaneously to different populations of sensory receptor (usually in different sense organs). The two stimuli would not normally be simultaneously present in the natural world. In the case of vision, two completely different images are presented to two eyes. In hearing, two tones differing in pitch are presented to the two ears. In smell, two entirely different odor compounds are presented to the two nostrils (Zhou & Chen, 2009). All of these stimuli produce the same kind of perceptual experience. Perception switches repetitively but unpredictably between the two alternatives. One image, tone, or odor dominates for a while, before being replaced by the other. Evidence again indicates that both adaptation and top-down feedback contribute to the alternation between the two perceptions in rivalrous stimuli, though this is an ongoing area of research (e.g. Tong et al., 2006).

Impoverished stimuli

Another strategy for exploring the role of top-down information flow in ambiguity resolution is to study the perception of impoverished stimuli. These stimuli contain so little information that it may be difficult or impossible to impose any interpretation at all without additional knowledge.

A number of studies have used visual images called Mooney faces (see Figure 7.6), named after the Canadian researcher, Craig Mooney,

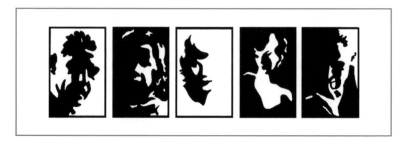

Figure 7.6 Impoverished images known as Mooney faces. They contain so little information that it is often difficult to reach a meaningful interpretation without some specific guidance. From Mooney (1957)

who devised them in the 1950s as a way to study the development of perception in infants (Mooney, 1957). Most observers have difficulty in recognizing some Mooney faces as faces. Neuroimaging data reveal that correct interpretations of Mooney faces are correlated with activity in an area of secondary visual cortex that seems to specialize in face processing, so these stimuli obviously recruit relatively high-level visual processes. An interesting aspect of Mooney face perception is that once the initially disorganized collection of white blobs in a particular image has been successfully combined into a meaningful percept, the whole image then takes on an apparently coherent structure. Each time that image is revisited the structure is immediately apparent. This change offers an opportunity to explore the role of top-down information flow. What happens to activity in the occipital lobe, where lower level processing takes place, once a Mooney image has been identified? If low-level processing occurs in an autonomous, bottom-up fashion, then there should be no difference in activation before and after recognition. On the other hand, if high-level signals reach down to steer low-level processing, then one would expect to see a difference. Hsieh *et al.* (2010) used a novel fMRI protocol to find the answer to this question. They compared the cortical activation pattern evoked by an impoverished Mooney face before and after an observer had been shown a richly detailed photographic version of the same face. Hsieh *et al.* (2010) found that the activation pattern in occipital cortex evoked by the Mooney face changed after the photograph had been viewed, so that it became more like the activation produced by the photograph itself. The fact that knowledge of object identity affects representation in occipital cortex is clear evidence for top-down information flow.

So there is accumulating evidence from psychophysical and neuro-imaging studies that perceptual representations involve both feed-forward signals from low-level processing areas of cortex to high-level areas, and feedback from high-level areas down to lower level areas. What role does this feedback loop play in sensory processing? As you saw in Figures 7.1 and 7.2, incoming sensory information is inherently ambiguous, though this ambiguity is not normally apparent at a subjective level. Somehow the brain manages to sift out all of the false interpretations of the sensory data, and preserve the correct interpretation. Given that the incoming data are not sufficient alone, the brain must bring in additional information that helps it to solve the problem. This additional information takes

Key Term

Occipital lobe. One of the four lobes of the cerebral cortex, known to be devoted to sensory processing of visual information.

the form of constraints or assumptions, in-built knowledge about the properties of real-world objects and scenes as was discussed earlier in the context of Marr's theory of vision, which limit the range of plausible interpretations. Some interpretations are far more likely to be true than others, and the brain selects the most likely or optimal real-world interpretation based on these prior expectations. Cortical feedback loops play a crucial role in applying these expectations to incoming sensory data.

Bayesian theories of ambiguity resolution

Bayes' theorem

A theorem known as **Bayes' theorem** provides the mathematical basis for modern theoretical accounts of ambiguity resolution in sensory processing. Unlikely as it seems, the theorem comes from an eighteenth-century English clergyman, the Reverend Thomas Bayes. In 1763 he published a highly influential mathematical theory of inductive logic, a type of reasoning in which a general conclusion is drawn from a specific set of facts; for example 'All the swans I have seen are white, therefore all swans are white'. Inductive inferences clearly underlie much of scientific reasoning. Bayes devised a simple mathematical formula for calculating the probability that a hypothesis is true, based on combining a prior estimate of its probability with new evidence about the hypothesis. The formula is very general, and can be applied to all kinds of hypotheses, including 'perceptual' hypotheses about real-world objects and scenes. In the case of the image in Figure 7.2, for example, many hypothetical objects are consistent with it, some of which are shown in the figure. To calculate the probability that any one hypothesis is true, the brain needs prior knowledge about the prevalence of the different shapes in the world ('**priors**'), as well as evidence derived from the incoming sensory data, which corresponds to the **likelihood** that each shape could create the image seen in Figure 7.2. Given that cuboid shapes are quite common in a modern visual environment (books, bricks, houses) and parallel lines in images are often created by objects with parallel edges, the brain may select the cube as the most likely interpretation of the image in Figure 7.2.

Key Terms

Bayes' theorem. A mathematical formula for drawing inferences by combining different sources of evidence, such as current information and past experience.

Prior. A probability value used in Bayesian inference, which estimates the probability of a particular interpretation on the basis of prior information (experience).

Likelihood. A probability value used in Bayesian inference, which estimates the probability of a particular interpretation on the basis of current sensory information.

Bayesian inference in perception

Bayesian inference is the cornerstone of modern theories about how the brain draws perceptual inferences, as illustrated in the functional block diagram in Figure 7.7. The computational goal of Bayesian theories is to calculate the most reliable estimate of a feature or object in the face of uncertain sensory information. Incoming sensory data supply information on the likelihood (relative probabilities) of different possible features or objects, given the data. In-built knowledge supplies the prior probability of each feature or object, based on experience. The likelihoods and priors are combined using Bayes' theorem to compute the probability associated with each interpretation, called the **posterior probability**. A decision on the most plausible interpretation can be made on the basis of the posterior probabilities. A simple rule is to select the interpretation that has the greatest probability, usually called the **maximum posterior probability** (or *maximum a posteriori probability*; abbreviated as **MAP**). The posterior probabilities may be refined by feeding the interpretations back down to lower level processes to test how well they fit the data. Adjusted likelihoods then feed forward to refine the interpretations. Bayesian theories of this kind show that perception is a trade-off between prior knowledge and the reliability of incoming data. With very reliable incoming data there may be relatively little need to invoke prior knowledge. In the case of very ambiguous data perception may rely much more on prior knowledge, and may even be unable to settle on a single definitive interpretation (as in the case of bistable stimuli).

How could a Bayesian theory be implemented in the brain? A basic premise of Bayesian inference is that the brain represents perceptual information probabilistically,

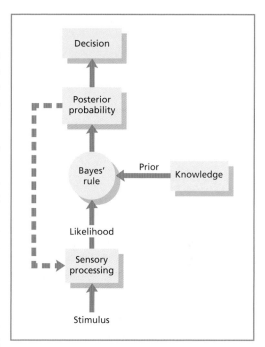

Figure 7.7 Functional diagram for Bayesian inference in sensory processing. A decision about a feature or object in the world is based on optimal combination of sensory information (likelihoods) with knowledge (priors), using Bayes' rule.

Key Terms

Posterior probability. The probability that a particular interpretation is correct, based on combining prior and likelihood values for that interpretation.

Maximum posterior probability (MAP). A rule for selecting among alternative interpretations, based on comparing their posterior probabilities and selecting the maximum among them.

KEY CONCEPT

Bayes' theorem

Although the derivation of Bayes' theorem is quite mathematical, the basic idea is simple. The aim is to draw an inference based on evidence from two sources, a prior and a likelihood. Let's take the example shown in Figure 7.2. The image on the retina, shown at the bottom, could have arisen from several possible objects, three of which are shown above. Let's assume for simplicity that these are the only possible interpretations. Prior experience has taught you about the properties of natural objects, and on this basis one of the candidate shapes is more plausible than others: the cuboid is far more plausible than the other shapes because it is frequently encountered in a modern environment (e.g. books, bricks). The mathematical term for this prior probability is P(S). The other source of evidence is provided by the sensory data. The likelihood that the image could have arisen from each object is labeled P(I/S). Many factors in images, such as occlusion and unusual viewpoints, can all impact on likelihood values associated with alternative interpretations. In this example the presence of parallel lines in the image is good evidence that the object has parallel edges. The table below summarizes the prior and likelihood values associated with each possible object in the example.

Shape	Prior P(S)	Likelihood P(I/S)	Posterior P(S/I)
A	0.1	0.05	0.005
B	0.1	0.05	0.005
C	0.8	0.9	0.72

Bayes' theorem combines them as follows:

$$P(S/I) \approx P(S) \times P(I/S)$$

The prior is multiplied by the likelihood to calculate the probability associated with each interpretation, known as the *posterior probability*, P(S/I). (The 'approximately equal' symbol '$\approx$' is used because a constant has been omitted from the equation for the sake of simplicity.) A simple rule for selecting an interpretation is to pick the interpretation that is most likely, known as the *maximum posterior probability* or *MAP*. In this example the MAP rule would select the cuboid shape.

in terms of codes that store the relative probabilities of alternative possible values for particular features or objects (the likelihoods and priors shown in Figure 7.7). Population codes are ubiquitous in sensory processing, and can be viewed as storing the relative probabilities of different stimulus values; the most probable values lie near the peak of the distribution. So according to the Bayesian scheme, a population code holding likelihood values is combined with a population code holding priors to compute the most likely perceptual hypothesis. This computational framework has been used successfully to explain a range of motion illusions (Weiss *et al.*, 2002) and brightness illusions (Jaramillo & Pearlmutter, 2006).

The hierarchical structure of processing in the sensory cortex is consistent with a Bayesian processing hierarchy (Lee & Mumford, 2003). Figure 7.8 summarizes cortical processing in vision, the best

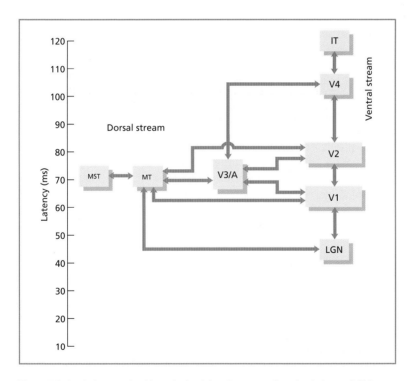

Figure 7.8 Cortical processing hierarchy for vision. Responses from the thalamus (LGN) pass through a series of areas involving successively higher levels of analysis. Each area has reciprocal connections with both higher and lower level areas. The vertical position of each box gives the latency of the initial response in each area after the onset of a stimulus. The relative size of the boxes approximates relative cortical area.

understood modality. It is well known that signals pass back and forth between a series of cortical areas. Responses emerge at higher cortical levels 120 milliseconds after the appearance of a visual stimulus, though they arrive at primary visual cortex within 60 milliseconds of the onset of stimulation. Cells in lower level areas such as V1 respond to simple stimulus features such as line orientation, while cells in higher level areas such as IT respond to more complex images such as geometrical shape and faces. The reciprocal connections between successive stages of processing show that information flows in both directions, as required for the Bayesian scheme in Figure 7.7. Notice that processing seems to divide into two interconnected branches or streams. The ventral IT stream may be involved in form and object perception, while the dorsal MST stream may focus on visually guided action (the dorsal/ventral distinction mentioned in previous chapters).

A recent neuroimaging study (Fang *et al.*, 2008) provides evidence that highly structured perceptual interpretations minimize activity in lower level cortical areas, consistent with Bayesian inference. Participants viewed a series of visual images that all contained the same set of lines, but in different spatial arrangements. In one image the lines were arranged in an unstructured, apparently random way, while in another image they were arranged to create a coherently structured object. Fang *et al.* (2008) used fMRI to compare activity in low-level and high-level visual cortex in the presence of the different images. The unstructured image evoked greater activity in low-level cortex than in high-level cortex, but the structured image had the opposite effect; less activation in low-level cortex. A plausible explanation for this result is that once an interpretation has emerged, cortical feedback serves to suppress any activity in lower level cortex that is not consistent with it.

A different perspective on the function of top-down signals is that they promote coding efficiency. Activation in high-level cortical areas is relatively sparse compared to the dense population codes in low-level areas, because high-level cells code global stimulus properties while low-level cells code more primitive, and numerous, local properties. Once the high-level representation evoked by a stimulus becomes active, the population codes in lower level cortical areas from which it was derived are no longer needed. They become redundant. So in the interests of coding efficiency and energy conservation, it would make sense for high-level cortical cells to send descending signals to attenuate redundant responses in low-level areas. Perhaps the suppression of low-level activity in Fang *et al.*'s (2008) study reflects the removal of redundant responses. Bayesian inferences may go hand in hand with coding efficiency. Reduced activation in low-level cortex is an inevitable consequence of Bayesian inference, since it selects among alternative interpretations. Minimization of ambiguity necessarily maximizes coding efficiency.

Bayesian inference in cue combination

Although signals at early levels of sensory processing provide the essential raw data for all higher levels of processing, they are tightly bound to stimulus properties that do not reflect important real-world properties. For instance, retinal image size and shape change drastically with variations in viewpoint, yet the brain must compute from these data a representation that reflects stable object dimensions rather than transient image properties. A bicycle, for example, does not appear to collapse in on itself when you view it from the front rather than from the side. Visual receptive fields are tied to retinal coordinates, yet the brain needs to compute object locations in a world-based coordinate system that remains fixed despite changes in the retinal image caused by eye and head movements. Similarly location signals from auditory cells tuned to inter-aural timing or level differences are fixed in head coordinates, yet the brain needs to compute stable sound source direction despite changes caused by head rotation. If an approaching cyclist sounds their bell, and you turn to look at them, any visual or auditory mislocalization caused by head rotation could have distinctly uncomfortable consequences.

The perceptual systems are quite adept at solving these problems. Many aspects of perception do indeed remain relatively stable in the face of drastic changes in the incoming data. For example, the apparent size of an object remains fixed despite large variations in retinal image size caused by variations in viewing distance. Middle C has the same apparent pitch whether played on a piano or on a flute, despite variations in the overtones or harmonics produced by the two instruments. These stable perceptions are called the perceptual constancies. How are they created and maintained?

One can view the problem of creating a relatively stable perceptual representation of a sensory object as an inference problem. Some aspects of the incoming sensory data reflect stable object properties, and others reflect transient extraneous factors in the sensory environment, such as viewing position. The sensory systems must separate out these two sources of variation, and infer constant object properties in the face of variable sensory data. The key to solving the problem is that multiple sources of information are usually available, and can be combined to draw stable inferences. For example, visual judgments of object size require information about retinal image size, visual cues as to the distance of the object from the observer, and may also use stored knowledge about the object. Estimates of pitch in the auditory system rely on timing cues in the firing pattern of auditory nerve fibers, as well as information in the pattern of responses across fibers. Variations in stimulus conditions often affect these different cues in different ways; some cues may disappear, or become unreliable, while other cues become very strong. In the case of visual size estimates, for instance, depth cue availability is very variable. In some conditions there are strong perspective cues to depth, such as converging lines or texture gradients, whereas in other conditions there may be weak perspective cues but strong motion cues from relative motion. In the case of pitch perception, some sounds offer reliable timing cues whereas others do not. Perception therefore involves flexible integration of information from different cues that takes account of cue reliability. Bayesian inference comes into play here. Cue reliability is stored in the likelihood information supplied by each cue. When the cues are combined to produce a best estimate of the stimulus they are each weighted according to their reliability (e.g. Hillis et al., 2004).

A specific example may make the argument a little clearer. When sliding a finger across a bumpy surface, finger position conforms to surface geometry. At the same time the force applied to the finger reflects the slope of the surface. So the sense of touch provides both a position cue and a force cue about the curvature of the surface. Drewing and Ernst (2006) explored how these two cues are combined to determine apparent surface curvature. They used a force-feedback device to create touch percepts from virtual objects: 'The virtual surface feels somewhat like a piece of rubber spread with liquid soap sensed through a thimble' (p. 94). Drewing and Ernst (2006) independently varied the reliability of the two cues, and found that perceived curvature was based on a combination of the two that was weighted by their reliability. Similar weighted combinations have also been found using visual stimuli that combine different visual depth and shape cues.

Evaluation

All sensory information is uncertain and ambiguous, so perception is inevitably a process of inference. It is tempting, but rather superficial and anthropomorphic, to equate perceptual hypotheses with intelligent problem solving in which the brain is compared to a detective who

Why do people drive too fast when visibility is poor?

Many drivers use excessive speed in foggy weather, despite the poor visibility, resulting in many serious road traffic accidents. Fog reduces the contrast between the lighter and darker regions of the visible scene. Laboratory studies have found that patterns appear to move more slowly at lower contrast (Thompson, 1982). Snowden *et al.* (1998) used a virtual-environment driving simulator to test whether a reduction in image contrast causes drivers to increase vehicle speed, consistent with an attempt to compensate for a reduction in apparent velocity. They found that experimental participants who were asked to drive at a certain speed drove faster at lower image contrasts (simulating foggier conditions), as expected on the basis of the laboratory studies. In another laboratory study, Gegenfurtner *et al.* (1999) compared speed perception in conditions designed to selectively activate rod and cone photoreceptors. They found that apparent speed in rod-mediated vision was lower than that in cone-mediated vision, and suggested that in the reduced visibility conditions of night-time driving drivers may underestimate their speed and hence drive too fast.

Why does low contrast or reduced visibility cause speed underestimation? Stocker and Simoncelli (2006) developed a Bayesian model of the effect. Their scheme includes a prior assumption that slower motions are more likely to occur than faster motions, which is combined with a population code for the velocity of motion in the image under view. In the model, perceived speed is intermediate between the prior speed and the speed signaled in the population code. A crucial feature of the model is that the population code becomes relatively unreliable at low contrasts, because of the variability in neural responses, so the Bayesian inference is weighted heavily in favor of the slow-speed assumption at low contrast, resulting in speed underestimation. Stocker and Simoncelli (2006) tested a prediction from the model, namely that participants' uncertainty about speed should increase as contrast decreases as a reflection of the unreliable population code. They found that the model fitted psychophysical data well over a wide range of stimulus parameters. Stocker and Simoncelli's (2006) assumption regarding a prior favoring slower motion is consistent with measurements from natural images, which find slower speeds more prevalent than faster speeds (Roth & Black, 2007). Their model therefore represents a plausible and testable application of Bayesian inference to perceptual judgments, which has broad applicability across the senses. On the other hand, Hammett *et al.* (2007) argue that the effect of contrast on apparent speed can be explained in terms of bottom-up processes in the visual cortex, without the need to invoke Bayesian 'priors'.

solves a crime by assembling and assessing evidence. Modern theories based on Bayesian inference advocate a rigorous, quantitative inferential model of perception that does not require the intuition and guesswork implied by comparisons with detectives.

According to modern Bayesian theories of perception, ambiguity is resolved by combining probabilistic bottom-up sensory responses held in low-level population codes with top-down perceptual hypotheses or inferences generated at higher levels of sensory processing. The notion of perception as hypothesis testing has quite a long history. It was first articulated clearly by the German physiologist Hermann von Helmholtz in the late 1800s. Helmholtz felt that perceptual inferences were analogous to the calculations made by an astronomer 'who computes the positions of the stars in space, their distances, etc.' from his conscious knowledge of the laws of optics; 'there can be no doubt', Helmholtz argued, that perception involves the same kind of computation as that used by the astronomer, but at an unconscious level (Helmholtz, 1910).

A limitation of the Bayesian approach is that it is a rather descriptive one. It describes how the computations work, but it does not explain why. In particular, it describes how constraints can be applied to incoming data to resolve ambiguity, but it does not tell us exactly what constraints should be used, and why. Many Bayesian models chose prior distributions on the basis of simplicity or computational convenience. The challenge for Bayesian theories is to generate priors based on computational considerations of the task at hand, or on measurements of the natural environment. A similar issue arose concerning the constraints built into Marr's theory of vision. Marr (1982) suggested that answers as to which constraints are used should be sought in everyday experience, psychophysical demonstrations, or even neurophysiological findings. More recent studies of the statistical properties of natural images provide another source of information about possible constraints or priors that may be exploited by the sensory systems.

Summary

- Sensory data are inherently ambiguous, so a core function of higher level neural processing is ambiguity resolution.
- Ambiguity could be resolved either by bottom-up competition between alternative interpretations, or by top-down imposition of perceptual hypotheses, or a combination of both.
- Researchers study ambiguity resolution in the brain using bistable, rivalrous, and impoverished stimuli. Results of physiological, psychophysical, and neuroimaging studies indicate that both bottom-up and top-down processes are used to resolve ambiguity.
- Bayesian theories in which sensory data are combined with assumptions based on experience offer a rigorous account of the interplay between bottom-up and top-down processing.
- Bayesian inference can also explain how information from different sensory cues is combined to produce relatively stable perceptual representations from variable sensory data.

REFLECTIVE EXERCISE

1. Which of the following has not been used to study the distinction between bottom-up and top-down processing in perception:
   a. Necker cube
   b. Mooney faces
   c. Verbal transformation
   d. Metamers

2. Discuss how processes that incorporate Bayesian inference might explain perceptual illusions.

3. On the basis of what you have learnt about perception, what could be done to reduce the chances of serious road traffic accidents in conditions of poor visibility?

FURTHER READING

- Glennerster, A. (2000) Computational theories of vision. *Current Biology*, *12*, R682–R685.
- Kersten, D., & Yuille, A. (2003) Bayesian models of object perception. *Current Opinion in Neurobiology*, *13*, 150–158.
- Knill, D.C., & Pouget, A. (2004) The Bayesian brain: the role of uncertainty in neural coding and computation. *Trends in Neurosciences*, *27*, 712–719.
- Lee, T.S., & Mumford, D. (2003) Hierarchical Bayesian inference in the visual cortex. *Journal of the Optical Society of America A*, *20*, 1434–1448.
- Sterzer, P., Kleinschmidt, A., & Rees, G. (2009) The neural bases of multistable perception. *Trends in Cognitive Sciences*, *13*, 310–318.

Multi-sensory processing

8

What this chapter will teach you

- How can the brain benefit from multi-sensory processing?

- What evidence is there for multi-sensory effects in perception?

- What physiological mechanisms mediate multi-sensory integration?

- What is synesthesia, and how can it be explained?

Introduction

Each of the sensory modalities, namely vision, hearing, touch, balance, taste, and smell, is served by its own sensory system, comprising a specialized set of receptor cells, pathway, and cortical receiving area. Anatomical and physiological segregation of the senses is beneficial because it avoids the confusion that would otherwise reign if they were merged at an early stage. It has also allowed the structures in each system to evolve optimal coding strategies for each modality.

Segregation does, however, have a major drawback. If each modality-specific system processes information independently of the other systems, then potentially useful information is discarded. Stimulation in the natural environment does not necessarily respect the subdivisions imposed by the nervous system. Natural objects frequently offer signals to multiple sensory systems simultaneously. A tumbling rock usually makes a sound as well as visual movement, a flying insect such as a mosquito can be seen, heard, and felt when it lands. A given food has a characteristic color, texture, smell, and taste. Because the information in each sensory modality often comes from a common source in the immediate environment, it is inevitably highly correlated in space and in time; you hear a rock fall from the same direction and at the same time as you see it fall.

According to information theory, if signals in different sensory systems are highly correlated then processing efficiency is best served by merging the signals together in some way. Such cross-modal integration would help to minimize redundancy and maximize signal reliability. The crucial questions for research on perception are whether and how this integration takes place. In principle integration could occur either at a post-perceptual *decision* stage where responses are selected and executed, or alternatively it could occur earlier in processing at the *perceptual* stage. Decision integration is illustrated in Figure 8.1a: Independent processing modules serving different sensory modalities offer information that can be used to select an appropriate response to the stimulation. Multi-modal stimulation necessarily provides more information on which to base a decision than uni-modal stimulation and can therefore result in better performance. For example, multi-modal information at the decision stage may allow a decision to be reached more quickly or with greater reliability. The alternative form of integration, perceptual integration, is illustrated in Figures 8.1b and 8.1c: Incoming signals in different modalities interact during perceptual processing itself, so that multi-modal stimulation boosts the strength of the signal in each modality in a similar way to increasing the strength of a uni-modal stimulus. Two variants of perceptual integration are shown in the figure. In one variant, vertical perceptual integration (Figure 8.1b), low-level modality-specific signals ascend to a higher order perceptual processing stage, which combines the signals into a multi-modal signal that is fed to the decision stage. In the other variant, horizontal perceptual integration

Key Term

Information theory. A branch of mathematical theory concerned with the efficiency with which information can be transmitted through a processing system; see Chapter 5.

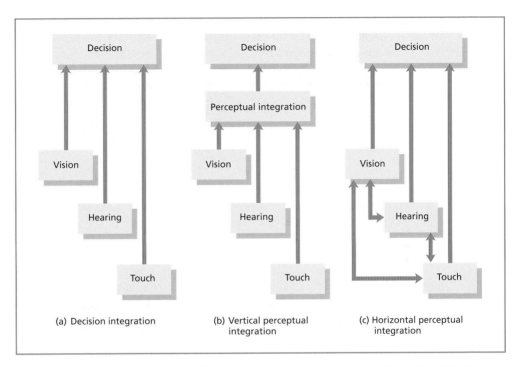

Figure 8.1 Possible schemes for cross-modal integration. (a) Integration occurs after perceptual processing, when responses are selected and executed; (b) vertical perceptual integration at a poly-sensory processing stage; (c) horizontal perceptual integration between modality-specific modules.

(Figure 8.1c), some signal energy is shared between the early modality-specific modules before they each send signals to the decision stage. Any or all of the three schemes depicted in Figure 8.1 could actually be implemented in the central nervous system for particular combinations of sensory signals. A hybrid scheme that includes both vertical and horizontal perceptual integration is also a possibility. A large number of psychophysical and physiological experiments have been conducted to establish which processing scheme is involved in specific perceptual decisions.

Psychophysical studies of multi-sensory processing

Many experiments have found evidence for multi-sensory processing, but it turns out to be very difficult to design experiments that distinguish definitively between simple decisional integration and true perceptual interaction. The standard experimental technique is to ask a participant to make a perceptual decision or judgment based either on uni-modal sensory information or on bi-modal information. Any difference in results between the two conditions should say something about how information is combined across the modalities. Experimental studies can be divided into those making quantitative measurements (typically threshold sensitivity), and those reporting qualitative, phenomenological effects of multi-modal stimulation.

Quantitative studies of threshold sensitivity

A commonly used experimental protocol involves measuring a participant's sensitivity to very weak stimulation in order to assess whether detectability improves when multiple sensory signals are available. For example, an experiment may test whether sensitivity is improved when both visual and auditory information are available (bi-modal) rather than just one or the other (uni-modal). Thresholds were discussed in Chapter 4 (p. 59). For the sake of argument let's assume that an experiment measured threshold sensitivity for a weak signal that could be either a visual flash, or an auditory tone, or both stimuli together. If sensitivity improves in the bi-modal condition one can conclude that some kind of multi-modal processing took place, but one cannot necessarily attribute that improvement to perceptual integration rather than decisional integration. The reasoning runs as follows. Let's assume for simplicity that the stimuli have been set up so that the participant has only a 50:50 chance of detecting either the flash or the beep when they are presented separately, so in each case the chance of detection is basically the same as the chance of getting heads in a single coin toss, 1/2. When both stimuli are presented together, the participant has two chances at detection rather than one (two coin tosses), so performance should improve significantly on purely statistical grounds. In fact the probability of detecting the joint stimulus should improve to 0.75. To see why this is so, consider the possible outcomes of two coin tosses. There are four: tails–tails, tails–heads, heads–tails, and heads–heads. So the probability of getting at least one head is 3/4 or 0.75. This kind of improvement in performance is called **probability summation**. It is a statistical effect that occurs at the decision stage (Figure 8.1a) where different signals

Key Term

Probability summation. A statistical effect in which the detection rate of a signal improves as the number of opportunities to detect it increases.

are combined to reach a detection decision. If performance in a multi-sensory task improves by more than the amount predicted by probability summation then one can begin to consider the possibility of perceptual integration, but even then the result is not definitive. The improvement may reflect changes in the way information is used in the decision stage. For example, multi-modal stimulation may cause the observer to change their response strategy, to alter the way sensory data inform their decision-making. In a multi-modal situation they may rely on less information in any one modality. Strategic changes of this kind are sometimes called shifts in 'response criterion'.

Given the potentially large impact of subtle variations in procedure on response strategy, it is not surprising that multi-modal studies of threshold sensitivity have produced mixed results. In some cases performance is no better than expected on the basis of probability summation; in other cases it is better than expected, but shifts in response criterion cannot be ruled out. For instance, several studies have investigated detection of movement using either visual stimuli, auditory stimuli, or audio-visual stimuli. Some studies have found no advantage for bi-modal presentation over and above that offered by probability summation (e.g. Wuerger *et al.*, 2003), while others report small but consistent effects (e.g. Sanabria *et al.*, 2007).

Qualitative studies of phenomenological judgment

Dramatic evidence of cross-modal interaction comes from experiments that involve phenomenological judgment of a particular perceptual quality. The most famous example is an effect called the McGurk effect, in which the speech sound heard by a listener is influenced by visual observation of the speaker's lips (McGurk & MacDonald, 1976). For example, if the sound is 'baa', but lip movements are consistent with saying 'gaa', the observer may report hearing 'daa' when they can see the lips, but 'baa' when they cannot. Ventriloquism is another well-established cross-modal phenomenon. Ventriloquists make their voice appear to come from elsewhere, usually a dummy head. The effect has been known since antiquity.

> ### DISCUSS AND DEBATE
>
> Ventriloquism goes almost unnoticed when you watch television and movies. Next time you are watching television, notice that sounds appear to emanate from a location inside the screen area (voice sounds appear to emanate from the actors' lips) rather than the speakers positioned at the side of the screen. Try closing your eyes while watching, to test whether the apparent location of the sound changes.

There are many other examples of cross-modal effects on perceived quality. Sounds heard while the hands are rubbed together can alter the perception of skin texture (Jousmaki & Hari, 1998); the strawberry smell of a liquid appears stronger when the liquid is colored red (Zellner & Kautz, 1990); food color may affect judgments of flavor or taste (Spence et al., 2010); two moving visual shapes may appear to collide if a noise is heard when they cross (Watanabe & Shimojo, 2001).

Phenomenological effects are very difficult to pin down in terms of causation. They could be a result of perceptual interaction or they could reflect decisional effects (response bias). Participants are fully aware of the stimuli, and can potentially decide to report whatever perceptual quality they like, regardless of the perceptual processing involved. Nevertheless many cross-modal effects behave in such a lawful way that it seems *plausible* to argue that they are a result of perceptual interactions.

Bayesian approaches to multi-sensory interaction

Each sensory modality provides a cue about a specific object property, such as its size or location, and these different cues must be combined in some way in order for an experimental participant to report a single estimate of the object property. The traditional view of how multi-sensory judgments are made is that one modality, usually vision, tends to capture or dominate the judgment. In other words, cues in different modalities are not really integrated at all. Recent theories based on Bayesian inference offer a more sophisticated perspective on multi-modal processing, which furnishes testable predictions.

In the previous chapter you saw how a sensory cue cannot provide totally reliable information about the world, but supplies only likelihood estimates attached to alternative interpretations. In a multi-sensory context, each sensory modality offers its own likelihood estimate for a particular object property. According to Bayesian theories the goal of cross-modal processing is to produce the most reliable and accurate single estimate from the multiple estimates that are available (see Figure 8.2). Bayesian inference predicts that the most reliable cues should have a greater influence on the final estimate, by virtue of their higher likelihood values. A good way to test this theory is to manipulate the reliability of the cues in different

Key Term

Bayesian inference. An inference drawn by combining different sources of evidence according to a rigorous mathematical formula; see Chapter 7.

modalities, and see whether there are consequent changes in the way that the cues are combined. One study looked at audio-visual cue integration in the perception of location (Alais & Burr, 2004). Participants were required to judge the location of small patches of light and brief auditory clicks, presented either separately or together. To assess cue integration, a conflict was introduced between the visual and auditory cues by displacing the position of one stimulus relative to the other. The reliability of the visual cue was manipulated by spatially blurring the patch of light so that it was spread over a large area. Unblurred light patches tended to dominate the location judgment in cue conflict conditions, consistent with the traditional view of visual capture. On the other hand, judgments made using blurred patches were dominated by the auditory cue, just as one would expect from optimal Bayesian combination.

Ernst and Banks (2002) investigated how visual and haptic (touch) cues are combined in order to judge object size. Subjects used stereo goggles to view a virtual-reality visual representation of a small block, while manually 'grasping' the object using a force-feedback device. They were asked to judge the width of the block on the basis of the visual and haptic information available. Like Alais and Burr, Ernst and Banks (2002) found that vision normally dominates this judgment. However, Ernst and Banks (2002) added varying amounts of jitter to the width of the visual stimulus to reduce its reliability, and found that judgments became more reliant on touch as visual cue reliability declined. As in the experiment by Alais and Burr (2004), the progressive change in cue weight was consistent with optimal Bayesian cue combination.

So experiments on cross-modal cue integration indicate that cues are combined very lawfully, in just the way predicted by theories of optimal Bayesian inference. How does the Bayesian framework in Figure 8.2 relate to the processing schemes in Figure 8.1? Higher order multi-modal areas (Figure 8.1b) seem an obvious candidate for

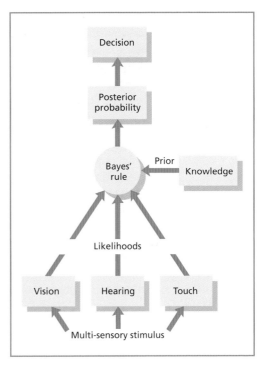

Figure 8.2 Bayesian inference in multi-sensory processing. Each modality-specific module supplies likelihood data that are combined with prior knowledge to produce a perceptual inference (posterior probability).

Bayesian integration of modality-specific cues. As you saw in the previous chapter, it may also be the case that multi-modal areas feed back down to modality-specific areas to steer their processing using perceptual inferences.

Physiological and anatomical evidence for multi-sensory processing

There is a wealth of physiological and anatomical evidence for interactions between the neural populations serving different sensory modalities, right down to the level of individual cells. Many sensory neurons in the brain are **multi-sensory**; they respond to stimulation either in a single sensory modality or in two or more modalities simultaneously. An important question is how their response changes when multi-sensory stimuli are presented. Research has shown that in some situations multi-sensory stimulation results in an enhanced response, and in other situations it results in response suppression. This modulation of response normally obeys three rules (Kayser & Logothetis, 2007):

- *Spatial coincidence* Many uni-modal sensory neurons have spatial receptive fields. For instance, in a visual neuron responses are restricted to stimuli falling within a small area of the visual field, and in an auditory neuron responses are limited to sounds emanating from a small range of directions. In multi-sensory neurons the receptive fields in different modalities normally overlap, and only stimuli falling inside the overlap area produce response modulation.
- *Temporal coincidence* Response modulation only occurs when stimuli in different modalities are presented in close temporal proximity; they arrive at approximately the same time.
- *Inverse effectiveness* The strength of response modulation depends on the degree to which each of the uni-modal stimuli drives the neuron's response. Stimuli that elicit a strong response tend to be immune to modulation in the presence of other stimuli, while stimuli that elicit a weak response show stronger interactions in the presence of other stimuli.

Key Term

Multi-sensory neuron. A sensory neuron that responds to stimulation in at least two modalities, such as vision and audition.

All of these effects indicate that the function of cross-modal interaction is to regulate responses according to the likelihood that they could have originated from the same source in the environment. Spatially and temporally coincident stimuli are more likely to have come from a common object, but relatively weak stimuli are less reliable than strong stimuli.

Key Term

Superior colliculus. A mass of neurons in the midbrain that is thought to be involved in integrating visual and auditory signals, and in directing visual attention.

You saw in the earlier chapters that all the sensory pathways contain relay stations en route from the periphery to the cortex. These relay stations offer side routes along which signals in one sensory modality can travel to interact with signals from another modality. The **superior colliculus** seems to be a particularly important destination. It contains cells responsive to visual, auditory, and somatosensory stimulation. Some neurons show 'superadditive' responses to multi-modal stimulation; their response to stimulation from multiple senses is much greater than the sum of their responses to each sense in isolation (Alvarado *et al.*, 2007). The superior colliculus is thought to be responsible for orienting the head and eyes towards salient objects in the environment.

Single-unit recording studies in the cortex have found multi-sensory cells in several higher order cortical areas, consistent with the scheme in Figure 8.1b (see Driver & Noesselt, 2008). As shown in Figure 8.3, these areas include an area in the temporal lobe called the superior temporal sulcus, and an area in the parietal lobe called intraparietal sulcus (IP). STP may construct multi-sensory representations of object identity, while IP may construct multi-sensory representations of object location and movement.

There is anatomical evidence from tracing studies that these higher order poly-sensory areas send feedback projections back down to modality-specific areas, as show in Figure 8.1b (Falchier *et al.*, 2002). There is also some sparse anatomical evidence for direct, lateral connections between early modality-specific cortical areas, consistent with the scheme in Figure 8.1c. Some anatomical studies in primate cortex have found direct connections between auditory cortex, visual cortex, and somatosensory cortex (Schroeder & Foxe, 2002). It is still not clear how significant these lateral connections are.

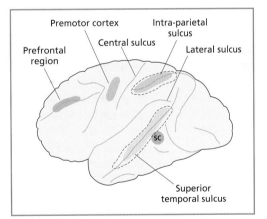

Figure 8.3 Cortical areas associated with sensory integration, as well as a subcortical structure, the superior colliculus (SC). Reproduced from Kayser (2007), with kind permission from Springer Science + Business Media.

Human neuroimaging studies show clear evidence of cross-modal interaction. For instance, it is well known that watching a speaker's lips during conversation (lipreading) improves speech perception (try listening to dialogue on television in a noisy room without watching the speaker's lips). Calvert *et al.* (1997) found that silent lipreading activated auditory cortical sites that are normally activated during perception of heard speech. Another study (Schurmann *et al.*, 2006) used fMRI to investigate integration of hearing and touch. Subjects heard bursts of noise, sometimes accompanied by tactile vibration applied to the fingers and palm. Responses to the sound in auditory cortex were enhanced in the presence of tactile stimulation.

In sensory-specific satiety, the pleasantness of a particular food decreases markedly after that food is eaten to satiety. This effect may explain why you may still have 'room for dessert' after eating a large main course, and why more food is eaten when a variety is available. Interestingly, sensory-specific satiety is specific to particular combinations of taste, smell, size, shape, and color. For instance, Rolls *et al.* (1982) found that after eating chocolate of one color the taste of chocolate in that color was rated as less pleasant than the taste of other colors, even though the chocolates differed only in appearance. A similar effect was found for pasta shapes. As discussed earlier, it is difficult to establish the neural substrate of phenomenological effects like this in sensory integration. They may reflect decisional integration. However, O'Doherty *et al.* (2000) measured sensory-specific satiety using both pleasantness ratings and fMRI. BOLD signals in response to presentation of banana or vanilla odor were recorded before and after participants had eaten banana to satiety. Pleasantness ratings of banana odor decreased significantly after eating banana, but there was no change in the rating of vanilla. The fMRI data showed that orbitofrontal cortex was activated by the odors, as expected (see Chapter 2). Crucially, BOLD activation in response to the banana decreased, while activation in response to vanilla did not (if anything it increased). So changes in orbitofrontal cortex clearly mirror the phenomenological effects in sensory-specific satiety. Indeed a single-unit recording study of sensory-specific satiety by Critchley and Rolls (1996) found that individual neurons in primate orbitofrontal cortex sensitive to the sight or smell of food decreased their response to the satiating food, and the effect tended to occur for all the sensory modalities to which the neuron responded.

The cross-modal effects found in neuroimaging studies could be mediated either by lateral connections in modality-specific cortex, or by vertical connections involving higher level poly-sensory areas, or both. Overall, physiological and anatomical evidence is consistent with Bayesian integration of information in different modalities, as described in the previous section. Cortical areas specific to each sensory modality provide evidence (likelihoods) that is combined in higher order poly-sensory areas to yield perceptual interpretations about multi-sensory objects. A feedback loop tests and refines the hypotheses.

Synesthesia

Synesthesia is an intriguing multi-sensory perceptual phenomenon in which only a single sensory modality is stimulated, but it evokes a sensory experience in two or more modalities (see Ward, 2008). For example, some people experience a color sensation not from visual stim-ulation, but from auditory stimulation. 'Colored hearing' is most commonly associated with speech sounds. Different sounds evoke different colors. There are also reports of color sensations evoked by non-speech sounds, by touch, and by smell. The most common type of synesthesia ('sensory union') involves ordered sequences such as numbers, letters, or days being perceived as sequences of colors: the letters A and E may evoke shades of red; I, M, and N evoke white; D evokes yellow; and so on. Numbers are similarly distinct in terms of color, as are musical sounds and certain words such as days of the week or city names.

Early doubts about the scientific worth of synesthesia were fueled by those who questioned whether it is a genuinely sensory phenomenon rather than learned associative pairings of colors and sounds, perhaps created while learning to read. Several lines of evidence rule out a simple learning account. Baron-Cohen *et al.* (1993) investigated the consistency of the pairings over time. Nine experimental subjects who reported synesthetic experiences were asked to report the colours evoked by 122 words, letters, and phrases. A matched group of control subjects were asked to spontaneously generate a color to associate with each stimulus, and encouraged to use a mnemonic to aid recall. Both groups were re-tested on 10% of the words, 1 year later in the case of the synesthetic experimental group, and 1 week later in the case of the control. Results showed 93% of the experimental group's color responses were identical on re-testing after a year, but only 37.6% of the control group's responses were identical after a week. Baron-Cohen *et al.* (1993) concluded that the phenomenon is a genuinely sensory one. Further evidence for the sensory nature of synesthesia comes from brain-imaging studies. Nunn *et al.* (2002) used fMRI to locate the cortical regions activated by speech in synesthetes and in control subjects. Synesthetes showed activation in area V4/V8 in the left hemisphere, a region normally activated by color. Control subjects showed no activation in V4/V8 when imagining colors in response to spoken words, despite extensive training on the association.

Synesthesia tends to run in families, and population studies indicate a genetic contribution, though the genes involved have not yet been identified (Baron-Cohen *et al.*, 1996). One study found a prevalence of 1 case of synesthesia in every 2000 people. Many more women than men reported synesthesia; the female:male ratio was 6:1. In one third of the cases there was a family history of synesthesia.

The most plausible account of synesthesia is that it involves direct neural connections between uni-modal cortical areas, of the kind that were discussed in the previous section. These connections may be weak or absent in the majority of the population, but enhanced genetically in synesthetes. The prevalence of associations between colors and words in synesthesia is consistent with this account, because the cortical regions responsible for vision and speech are located near to each other.

According to the theory of evolution, traits are transmitted to successive generations only when they confer an advantage on their host. What advantages might synesthetes possess? One suggestion is that synesthetes are more creative, and therefore more able to generate novel and adaptive ideas that promote survival and reproduction (artistic personalities are claimed to have more sexual partners). This idea is contradicted by studies that find no conclusive evidence for differences in creativity between synesthetic and control subjects. A more plausible account of the synesthetic advantage was offered by Yaro and Ward (2007), who compared memory in synesthetic and control subjects. In the learning phase of their experiment each subject was read a list of 15 words and then had to recall as many words as they could in any order. In the retention phase (up to 2 weeks later) the words were not presented again, and the subject had to recall as many as they could remember from the learning phase. Synesthetic subjects consistently recalled more words than control subjects in both the learning and retention phases of the experiment (see Figure 8.4). A small advantage in memory ability may be sufficient to sustain the synesthesia trait.

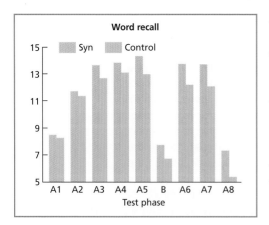

Figure 8.4 Results of a word recall experiment using synesthetic and control participants. Word list A was heard and recalled five times (A1–A5). Then list B was heard and recalled. Finally list A was recalled three times (A6–A8). Synesthetic participants performed slightly better than controls in all conditions.

Evaluation

There is now a wealth of perceptual evidence for multi-sensory processing, but it is often very difficult to distinguish between multi-modal *perceptual* interaction and an alternative account based on *decisional* integration. The most dramatic evidence comes from multi-modal effects on phenomenological judgments, such as perceived location, or speech perception. Phenomenological reports should always be treated with some caution, because one can never be sure of their origin (participants may report what they think the experimenter wants them to report). Nevertheless, many experiments show lawful, predictable variations in perceptual judgments when cue reliability is manipulated. These variations can be explained by a Bayesian theory of cross-modal interaction in which uni-modal cues are combined to produce multi-modal perceptual interpretations.

Physiological and anatomical evidence is consistent with the theoretical framework emerging from perceptual research. Higher order multi-modal cortical areas could perform Bayesian integration of uni-modal responses to construct multi-modal object hypotheses. A feedback loop between multi-modal and uni-modal areas may serve to refine the hypotheses, similar to the feedback loops discussed in the previous chapter.

RESEARCH QUESTION

Why do I experience motion sickness?

Most people have experienced motion sickness at some point in their life, usually while traveling in a car, airplane, or ship. Typical symptoms include light-headedness, lethargy, sweating, nausea, and perhaps vomiting; generally a rather unpleasant experience. Seventy percent of astronauts suffer motion sickness that starts in the first few hours of weightlessness and can last up to 96 hours (Lackner & DiZio, 2006).

Motion sickness can be attributed to sensory integration of signals in the visual system and the vestibular system. Both systems provide information about bodily movement. In the case of vision, the information comes from visual motion across the retina; in the case of the vestibular system the information comes from deflection of hair cells in the semi-circular canals, the saccule, and the utricle (described in Chapter 1). It seems that motion sickness occurs when there is a marked conflict between the motion signals generated by (and within) the two systems. Normally the signals obey three rules, and when any one of them is violated motion sickness is a likely consequence (Stott, 2002).

1 When rotational motion is sensed by the semi-circular canals, there should be an equivalent rotation of the visual scene in the opposite direction. This rule may be violated when you are inside a cabin with no view of the outside environment while the vessel in moving, so there is no visual motion corresponding to the vestibular signals.
2 When the head is tilted, the rotation sensed by the semi-circular canals should match the change in the direction of gravity sensed by the saccule and utricle. This rule may be violated while cornering in a vehicle or banking in an airplane. The force generated by the turn adds to gravitational force to create an erroneous signal for the direction of gravity.
3 The strength of the gravitational signal in the saccule and utricle normally fluctuates periodically during walking, as the head bobs up and down. Fluctuations that occur at much slower rates than the natural rate, such as those generated by ship movements at sea, can cause nausea.

Why should abnormal or mismatching visual and vestibular signals cause vomiting? One plausible theory on the evolutionary origin of motion sickness is that ingested neurotoxins may disturb sensory input or motor control, causing abnormal correlations between visual and vestibular signals. Vomiting evolved to rid the body of the toxins (Treisman, 1977). So motion sickness is an accidental by-product of this protective mechanism, which is triggered by modern transportation that takes the sensory systems outside their normal operating range. Alcohol can also be considered a toxin if it is ingested in large quantities; it alters the buoyancy of the crista, as mentioned in Chapter 1, resulting in nausea and vomiting (Money & Miles, 1974).

Summary

- Multi-sensory processing can take advantage of the correlation between signals in different modalities to improve processing efficiency and reliability.
- Many phenomenological and psychophysical experiments find evidence for multi-sensory effects in perception, but it is often difficult to distinguish between decisional integration and truly perceptual integration.
- Evidence for lawful interactions between multi-sensory cues is consistent with Bayesian perceptual integration.
- At a physiological level multi-sensory integration could occur in higher level poly-sensory cortical areas, via direct connections between lower level modality-specific areas, or via subcortical convergence. Evidence indicates that integration exploits all three routes.
- In synesthesia a multi-sensory percept is triggered by uni-sensory stimulation. The most plausible current explanation is that some individuals possess enhanced, direct neural connections between uni-modal cortical areas.

REFLECTIVE EXERCISE

1. Which of the following effects is not associated with multi-modal sensory processing:
   a. McGurk effect
   b. Rivalry
   c. Ventriloquism
   d. Superadditivity

2. Your friend says she can better understand what you are saying when she looks at you. Why might this be so?

3. Supermarkets are known to use color in shop lighting to increase sales (e.g. red near the meat counter). Why does this trick work?

FURTHER READING

- Burr, D., & Alais, D. (2006) Combining visual and auditory information. *Progress in Brain Research*, *155*, 243–258.
- Driver, J., & Noesselt, T. (2008) Multisensory interplay reveals cross-modal influences on 'sensory-specific' brain regions, neural responses, and judgements. *Neuron*, *57*, 11–23.
- Ernst, M.O., & Bulthoff, H.H. (2004) Merging the senses into a robust percept. *Trends in Cognitive Sciences*, *8*, 162–169.
- Schroeder, C.E., Smiley, J., Fu, K.G., McGinnis, T., O'Connell, M.N., & Hackett, T.A. (2003) Anatomical mechanisms and functional implications of multisensory convergence in early cortical processing. *International Journal of Psychophysiology*, *50*, 5–17.
- Ward, J. (2008) *Synesthesia*. Hove, UK: Psychology Press.

Consciousness and perception

9

What this chapter will teach you

- What is the difference between Cartesian dualism and identity theory?

- What techniques can be used to study the neural correlates of consciousness?

- What role might the thalamus play in consciousness?

- How does identity theory relate to epiphenomenalism in consciousness?

Introduction

Everyone feels that they know what consciousness is from first-hand experience: awareness of oneself and one's surroundings. Perceptual awareness of the world is undoubtedly one of the defining features of consciousness, so a book such as this on fundamental concepts in sensation and perception would be incomplete without a discussion of consciousness.

Consciousness is a fascinating but elusive and baffling phenomenon to study scientifically. Perceptual scientists largely ignore consciousness, taking it as given, because it is usually not relevant to the theories of sensory processing that they develop and test. Consciousness is the 'elephant in the room', a massive unresolved issue. Indeed some philosophers argue that the human mind can never get to the bottom of consciousness. According to this view, all minds have a limit as to what they can represent, a representational capacity. What is closed to a fly's mind may be open to a monkey's mind (if either of those creatures can be considered to have a mind). A monkey can use a stick to reach food that is just out of reach, but often a fly cannot even escape from a room by finding an open window. Perhaps human minds do not possess the representational capacity to grasp the true nature of consciousness (McGinn, 1993)? If this is the case then there is no alternative but to wait until humans evolve better brains, or until a sufficiently powerful non-human brain comes along. This view seems overly pessimistic, an excuse for doing nothing. There is much that can be done to explore the nature of consciousness, though admittedly there are as yet relatively few clear conclusions.

Mind and brain

According to the traditional philosophical view called **Cartesian dualism**, mind and matter are fundamentally different in nature; one does not depend on the other. Consequently one can exist without the other; the after-life, spirits, and reincarnation all follow on from dualism. Cartesian dualism is named after the French philosopher René Descartes, who believed that the spiritual world and the physical world communicated with each other via a special organ in the head, the pineal gland. Descartes chose the pineal gland because it is unique, whereas most other organs come in pairs. There is, of course, no scientific evidence that the pineal gland acts as a portal into the spirit world. Medical science has revealed that it secretes a hormone, melatonin, which controls diurnal rhythm: the 'body clock'.

Modern scientists do not generally accept Cartesian dualism as a plausible account of consciousness. They believe instead that consciousness is closely associated with activity in certain brain cells. This kind of theory is called **identity theory**. If conscious-

Key Term

Cartesian dualism. A philosophical tradition named after René Descartes, which posits that mind and brain are fundamentally different in kind; one cannot be reduced to the other.

ness can be identified with neural activity it follows that it cannot exist without active brain cells. There can be no after-life, no spirits, no reincarnation. If one accepts identity theory, as most scientists do, then a fundamental question immediately arises. *Which* brain cells generate consciousness? Psychologists and neuroscientists try to tackle this question by searching for **neural correlates of consciousness (NCC)**. Given the prominence of perception in ideas about consciousness, research has generally focused on finding the neural correlates of simple sensory experiences or qualia (loudness, brightness, heat, motion).

Key Terms

Identity theory. A theory that identifies consciousness with neural activity in the brain; all conscious events must have corresponding neural events.

Neural correlate of consciousness (NCC). The set of neural events that give rise to a specific conscious experience.

Qualia. Primitive conscious mental states, such as the felt quality of a color or a sound.

Neural correlates of consciousness

A neural correlate of consciousness, or NCC, can be defined as 'the minimal set of neuronal events that gives rise to a specific aspect of a conscious percept' (Crick & Koch, 2003). An example of a putative NCC in perception is that activity in the mid-temporal area of the cortex (MT) is the neural correlate of consciously experienced visual motion. How can such proposals be tested?

Testing for neural correlates of consciousness

Several empirical techniques can test for NCCs:

- Neuroimaging – Is the proposed neural system active during a percept?
- Clinical case studies – Does a lesion in the neural system impair the corresponding percept?
- Transcranial magnetic stimulation (TMS) – Does TMS interfere with the percept?
- Microstimulation – Does stimulation of cells influence a percept?

In the case of cortical area MT, there is very good evidence from all of these techniques that activity is closely associated with motion perception. Neuroimaging studies find changes in BOLD response in area MT following adaptation to motion, as you saw in Chapter 3 (Tootell *et al.*, 1995; see Figure 3.2, p. 45). Rare cases of akinetopsia (motion blindness) show that damage to cortical areas near MT abolishes the ability to perceive movement. One account of a patient who suffered akinetopsia following damage to area MT (Zihl *et al.*, 1983) described how she found it difficult to cross a road because she could not see vehicles as moving, though she had no difficulty in actually identifying the cars. Even simple tasks such as pouring tea were difficult because she could not sense the rising liquid in the cup. Face-to-face conversations were difficult because she could not lipread.

It may seem implausible to propose that activity in single neurons makes a measurable contribution to perceptual responses, but there is actually evidence to support it. Salzman *et al.* (1992) tested the proposal that cells in MT play a crucial role in motion perception. They trained monkeys to make a perceptual discrimination between two patterns containing moving dots. In each pattern only a proportion of dots moved consistently in a particular direction (as shown in Figure 4.6), and Salzman *et al.* (1992) measured how the monkey's performance varied as a function of the percentage of coherently moving dots in the pattern (shown by the open symbols in Figure 9.1). As coherence increased, the monkey's ability to perform the discrimination also increased. Then the experimenters found some cells in area MT of the animal's cortex that respond selectively to motion, and stimulated one of these individual cortical cells while the animal was actually performing the task. They found that the animals' judgments, as indicated by their behavioral responses, were influenced by the activity. The solid symbols in Figure 9.1 show discrimination performance during stimulation. Amazingly stimulation of individual cells was sufficient to bias the animal's perceptual decisions (the vertical axis shows the proportion of responses that accorded with the cell's preferred direction). One can speculate that stimulation influenced the perception of movement that accompanied each decision in the task.

In TMS (described in Chapter 3) an electric current is passed through a coil held against the scalp, to generate a brief, high-

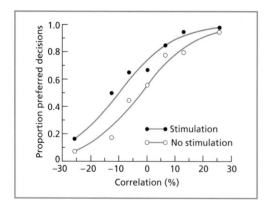

Figure 9.1 Psychophysical results of a microstimulation experiment on macaque monkeys. The monkey was taught to discriminate between two motion directions, using stimuli containing a variable percentage of correlated motion. Without stimulation (open symbols) performance rises as the consistency of the motion increases. When a cell in MT is stimulated during the task (filled symbols) psychophysical responses are biased to favor the direction that matches the preferred direction of the cell. Reprinted by permission from Macmillan Publishers Ltd: Salzman *et al.* (1990), copyright 1990.

intensity magnetic field. The field induces currents in the neural circuits below the location of the coil on the scalp. When TMS is focused over area MT it can produce a perception of moving lights, and can also interfere with performance in motion discrimination tasks (Sack *et al.*, 2006).

Consciousness, the cortex, and the thalamus

So area MT is closely associated with one small aspect of consciousness, the perception of motion. Other cortical areas are similarly associated with other percepts, such as colors, faces, sounds, and objects. Is consciousness distributed piecemeal across the whole of the cerebral cortices, or is there a certain area or neural circuit that is required for *general* conscious awareness? Humans can lose large chunks of cerebral cortex without a general loss of consciousness, but relatively small bilateral lesions in the thalamus are sufficient to completely destroy the capacity for conscious awareness (Bogen, 1995). Some researchers have suggested that activity in part of the thalamus, namely the intra-laminar nuclei (ILN), is an essential correlate of general awareness. The ILN are well placed to play a role in consciousness because many brain regions project to them, including those serving perception. Neuroimaging reveals that under general anesthesia the ILN is severely depressed, but there is no such depression in the cerebral cortex (White & Alkire, 2003). Two clinical cases also indicate that the thalamus plays a vital role in conscious awareness.

At 21 years of age Karen Ann Quinlan suffered a cardiac arrest after accidentally ingesting a combination of prescription sedatives and alcohol. She was unresponsive when found, with no pulse and dilated pupils. During the first week after resuscitation, she recovered responsiveness to stimulation, including flexion of the hands and feet, turning the head, yawning, grunting, and withdrawal from pinpricks. She had a sleep–wake cycle, but never showed signs of awareness of her environment nor any cognitive function. She remained in a persistent vegetative state for 10 years, eventually dying from overwhelming infection. Post-mortem analysis of her brain showed only focal damage to the cortex, with the brain stem regions serving arousal, sleep, autonomic, and respiratory control all being intact. On the other hand there was severe damage to the thalamus. Clinicians concluded that '. . . the disproportionately severe and bilateral damage in the thalamus as compared with the damage in the cerebral cortex supports the hypothesis that the thalamus is critical for cognition and awareness and may be less essential for arousal' (Kinney *et al.*, 1994, p. 1473).

The patient in the second clinical case was a 38-year-old man who sustained a closed head injury following a serious assault and, for a period of 6 years prior to treatment, remained in a minimally conscious state. This condition is characterized by intermittent evidence of awareness of self or the environment, but a failure to respond to commands and to communicate. The patient's cortex was relatively intact, so in this study (Schiff *et al.*, 2007) he was given bilateral deep brain stimulation of the central thalamus to investigate whether any residual functional capacity could be recovered. To measure changes in his state of awareness, the patient was assessed using a standard clinical instrument, the JFK Coma Recovery Scale. Scores without stimulation were compared against scores with stimulation switched on. The patient showed improved arousal, motor control, and responsiveness. Members of his family reported a significant recovery in his ability to interact consistently and meaningfully with others. Prior to stimulation the patient could not swallow or speak and rarely opened his eyes, although he sometimes appeared to mouth words. After stimulation he could feed himself, speak, recognize, and converse with family members.

Consciousness: Cause or effect?

Various perceptual functions such as wavelength discrimination and sound localization can be explained in terms of neural processes. The activation of these brain functions is accompanied by conscious experiences. When you see, you experience visual sensations; you feel the quality of redness, of a bright flash, of distance, and so on. When you hear, you feel the quality of a clarinet note, of a thunder clap, and so on. *Why* does visual or auditory experience accompany visual or auditory processing in the brain? Why not just have the visual or auditory processing?

Theories of causation in consciousness

The results of NCC studies support identity theory, in that they demonstrate an intimate link between specific brain activity and consciousness, but they cannot reveal *causation* in consciousness because they are, by definition, correlational. There are three alternative causal accounts of consciousness:

- Consciousness is causal; it drives our decisions and behaviors.
- Consciousness is a by-product of our decisions and behaviors; it does not cause them.
- Both consciousness and behavior are caused by a third agent.

Let's concentrate on the first two accounts, since the third is more at home in movies such as *The Matrix*. Figure 9.2 summarizes the difference between the two accounts. In the causal account, sometimes called **mental causation**, conscious experiences cause us to behave in certain ways. This account accords with everyday intuition; when I feel like a cup of coffee, I make one; when I feel an itch, I scratch it. In the alternative account consciousness does not cause behavior, but is a by-product or 'epiphenomenon' associated with the performance of other functions. Philosophers call this latter view of consciousness **epiphenomenalism**; when I scratch an itch, I feel it.

Mental causation implies that consciousness serves a function; certain decisions or behaviors would not be possible, or would not be executed so effectively, in the absence of consciousness. There are plenty of theories around that ascribe a causal function to consciousness. One theory argues, for instance, that it serves to integrate disparate pieces of information (Tononi, 2004), and another claims that it allows us to understand what other people are thinking about (Frith & Frith, 2007). However no one has been able to provide conclusive evidence in favor of any causal theory. A specific example will help to make the argument clearer. One theory posits that consciousness

> **Key Terms**
>
> **Mental causation**. A theory which posits that intentional mental states cause intentional actions.
>
> **Epiphenomenalism**. A theory which posits that consciousness is caused by neural activity, but has no causal influence on activity.

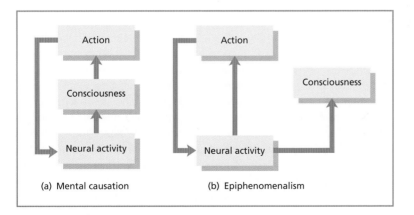

(a) Mental causation   (b) Epiphenomenalism

Figure 9.2 Two views of causation in consciousness. (a) Mental events cause behavior, though they are grounded in neural activity. (b) Mental events are by-products or epiphenomena of the neural events that cause behavior.

integrates disparate representations in different parts of the brain. Consciousness results from competition between alternative representations; the winner of the competition determines consciousness. The neural basis of the competition is supposed to be cells in the prefrontal cortex (see Maia & Cleeremans, 2005). However this theory, and others like it, side-steps the crucial issue. Why does activity in these cells lead to consciousness, but activity in other cells does not? As some of the supporters of this theory acknowledge themselves, 'It seems that it would be possible to have a system without qualia that would have the properties we outlined' (Maia & Cleeremans, 2005, p. 402). Competitive interactions between neurons, the interplay of excitation and inhibition, can be found everywhere in the central nervous system. There is no basis for associating some of these interactions with consciousness, and not others.

One can argue that the basic problem with causal accounts of consciousness arises from identity theory. If all conscious experience is ultimately embodied in neural activity, then it follows that any behavior that can be described in terms of conscious causation can equally well be described in terms of neural causation. The conscious element is superfluous, so one can dispense with the 'Consciousness' box in the chain of causation depicted in Figure 9.2a. The only way to accommodate both consciousness and identity theory is to treat consciousness as a mysterious by-product of neural activity, as shown in Figure 9.2b.

Experimental studies of causation in consciousness

Many experimental studies have actually produced evidence that is consistent with the view that consciousness follows on from decisions and behavior, as one would expect on the basis of epiphenomenalism, rather than precedes decisions and behavior as one would expect from mental causation. In some of these studies the participant is required to make an intentional action, manually pointing to a visual target. If the target unexpectedly jumps position after the action has been initiated, an appropriate movement correction can usually be made by the participant. However participants' awareness of the unexpected jump occurs more than 200 ms *after* the movement correction was initiated (Castiello & Jeannerrod, 1991). In other studies the experimental participant is instructed to lift their finger whenever they want, and to indicate the moment that they first had the urge to lift their finger by noting the position of a rapidly rotating hand on a clock face. The experimenter records brain activity throughout the procedure.

Remarkably, although the self-reported awareness of intent precedes the actual movement by about 200 ms, brain activity preparing for the movement precedes conscious report by about 350 ms (see the Research Question box). These results suggest that unconscious brain activity leads both to conscious experience of an intention to act and to the action itself.

Thus many studies show that your awareness of your own movements is an incomplete, delayed version of the actions carried out by your motor control circuits. Conscious intent does not appear to be the trigger for action. One could argue that control of action is governed by the dorsal processing stream that has been mentioned several times previously (see Figure 7.5), and that the dorsal stream does not serve conscious awareness. The ventral stream, on the other hand, does mediate conscious awareness. However this distinction still begs the question, why is awareness required in one stream and not the other?

Consciousness as a spandrel

There is no conclusive evidence that consciousness is causal, and several lines of evidence are consistent with the alternative explanation that it does not serve any essential function. If consciousness is an epiphenomenon, why does it exist at all? According to Darwin's theory of evolution, biological traits that improve the prospects of survival and reproduction are retained, and others die out. How is it possible to have evolved a salient property of the brain, namely consciousness, that is non-adaptive and serves no demonstrable function? There is evidence that evolution can in fact produce non-adaptive traits. The belly button, to take a trivial example, does not serve any adaptive function that anyone can discern, but is a by-product of an adaptation, the umbilical cord. Gould and Lewontin (1979) called such non-adaptive traits 'spandrels', after the architectural term. A spandrel in a building is the triangular-shaped space where a rounded arch or window meets a ceiling or dome (see Figure 9.3).

Spandrels are a by-product of the overall building design; the arches and domes were not designed deliberately to create them. If the design specifies a dome resting on arches, then spandrels will be created. Ornamentation can be applied to architectural spandrels to enhance the overall design, so the spandrel can take on a decorative function. To take another example, an internal combustion engine is designed to create turning force at the road wheels, but produces heat as an undesirable by-product that requires new design features (a

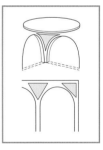

Figure 9.3 Spandrels. Top: A three-dimensional spandrel (pendentive) formed as the triangular space where a domed roof meets rounded arches. Bottom: Two-dimensional spandrels formed between rounded arches and a rectangular frame. From Gould (1997).

water jacket, water pump, and radiator). Car designers have made a virtue out of a necessity by using the heat generated by the engine to warm the passenger cabin. Evolutionary spandrels may also come to serve a function. Gould (1997) points out that extremely complex adaptations such as brains are likely to possess many spandrels. These spandrels may become very salient or dominant features of the organ by virtue of its capacity to co-opt them for new functions.

To establish the hypothesis that a trait is an evolutionary spandrel, one must identify the adaptation of which it is a by-product, and the reason for its association with the adaptation. The best one can say at present about current theories on the function of consciousness (such as the integration theory described earlier) is that they are really theories about the adaptations of which consciousness is a by-product. The fundamental question still remains unanswered: Why does consciousness exist?

Evaluation

A great deal of progress has been made in the search for neural correlates of conscious awareness, particularly with regard to perceptual awareness. Convergent evidence from a number of techniques has identified the cortical regions associated with very specific sensory experiences, as well as the brain structures associated with general awareness. However this is relatively safe ground. Theories about the *function* of consciousness have made comparatively little headway. If one accepts the proposal that consciousness is identified with neural activity in the brain, then there seems little option but to view it as an epiphenomenon. Such a view raises serious moral and legal issues concerning criminal responsibility, which have not yet been resolved (Greene & Cohen, 2004; Eastman & Campbell, 2006).

Epiphenomenalism still leaves open the question of how consciousness emerges as a mysterious by-product of neural activity. Perhaps the crux of the problem is that we do not really know what kind of a thing consciousness is. At least we are in good company. As the celebrated physicist Richard Feynman remarked: 'We have no knowledge of what energy is. We know how to calculate its value for a great variety of situations, but beyond that it's just an abstract thing.' (Feynman, 1998, p. 69). At least physicists have an empirical handle on energy – some measures and laws such as conservation of energy. In the case of consciousness there is still no universal agreement on how to define it, or on how we can measure it empirically.

RESEARCH QUESTION

Does consciousness precede willed actions?

Many people find epiphenomenalism unpalatable and counterintuitive. It is simply unacceptable to relegate such a fundamental aspect of the human condition to the status of an epiphenomenon. However, there is experimental support for the idea. In a widely cited experiment, Libet (1985) asked participants to make occasional, intentional finger movements while he recorded electrical potentials from the scalp. A well-known readiness potential (RP) was found to precede finger movements by around half a second, and this constitutes the brain activation that precedes voluntary action. Participants were also asked to indicate their initial awareness of their intention to act by reporting the position of a rapidly rotating hand on a clock face. Remarkably, this awareness followed the RP by about 350 ms. The delay indicates that the conscious experience of willing an action occurs *after* the brain events that set the action in motion.

Furthermore, actions can also occur with no experience of willing the action. In activities such as dowsing, divining, and Ouija-board spelling, participants are amazed that actions can occur spontaneously, without intentional effort on their part. However, careful measurements of the forces involved have confirmed that the participants did indeed initiate the actions (see Wenger, 2003).

Based on findings such as these, the 'theory of apparent mental causation' proposes that our experience of conscious will is merely an inference that thoughts cause actions, which does not necessarily bear any relation to the actual causes of actions (Wenger, 2003). Whether the theory is correct or not is a matter for empirical inquiry; introspection alone cannot provide an answer.

Summary

- Perceptual awareness is one of the defining features of consciousness.
- Cartesian dualism argues that mind and brain are fundamentally different, while identity theory argues that consciousness can be identified with neural activity in the brain.
- Modern neuroscientists accept identity theory, and search for the neural correlates of specific conscious experiences. An array of empirical techniques provide evidence to link particular patterns of activity to primitive mental states known as qualia.
- The intra-laminar nuclei of the thalamus appear to play a crucial role in maintaining general conscious awareness.
- If one accepts the truth of identity theory, the only way to accommodate consciousness in current views of brain function is that it is an epiphenomenon associated with activity in certain brain cells, which may have evolved as a by-product of some other adaptation.
- No one knows how consciousness arises from brain activity, and there are still fundamental disagreements on how to define and measure consciousness.

REFLECTIVE EXERCISE

1. Which of the following techniques is not used to study neural correlates of consciousness:
   a. Lesions
   b. Neuroimaging
   c. Neuroanatomy
   d. Transcranial magnetic stimulation

2. What role does cortical activity play in conscious experience?

3. According to evidence for epiphenomenalism, you do not really have conscious control of your actions. So are you really to blame when you break the law?

FURTHER READING

- Block, N. (2005) Two neural correlates of consciousness. *Trends in Cognitive Sciences, 9,* 46–52.
- Chalmers, D.J. (1995) Facing up to the problem of consciousness. *Journal of Consciousness Studies, 2,* 200–219.
- Eastman, N., & Campbell, C. (2006) Neuroscience and legal determination of criminal responsibility. *Nature Reviews Neuroscience, 7,* 311–318.
- Greene, J., & Cohen, J. (2004) For the law, neuroscience changes nothing and everything. *Philosophical Transactions of the Royal Society, B, 359,* 1775–1785.
- Pockett, S., Banks, W.P., & Gallagher, S. (eds) (2006) *Does Consciousness Cause Behavior?* Cambridge, MA: MIT Press.
- Rees, G., Kreiman, G., & Koch, C. (2002) Neural correlates of consciousness in humans. *Nature Reviews Neuroscience, 3,* 261–270.
- Schiff, N.D. (2008) Central thalamic contributions to arousal regulation and neurological disorders of consciousness. *Annals of the New York Academy of Sciences, 1129,* 105–118.

Summary and future directions 10

What this chapter will teach you

- What are the three levels of description used in theories of sensation and perception?

- What major issues remain to be resolved in perceptual science?

- What are the likely future applications of perceptual science to real-world problems?

Introduction

When you see, hear, touch, taste, or smell something, your experience is the culmination of a chain of events that starts in the sensory receptors and progresses through the billions of neurons that make up the parts of your nervous system that deal with sensory perception. The preceding chapters have considered this experience from a diverse range of empirical and theoretical perspectives. At this point I will step back from the detail and try to identify the major themes and issues that have emerged, and to think about the likely directions of future research.

Major themes

Levels of description

Scientists universally agree that sensation and perception are intimately linked with neural activity in the brain. Mental states correspond to physical states in the brain's neurons. A change in mental state, such as a change in one's perceptual experience, is always accompanied by a change in the pattern of neural activity in the brain. Following damage to certain neurons the corresponding mental states are altered or absent entirely. You have read, for example, about akinetopsia (p. 148) in which damage in extrastriate cortex selectively abolishes the ability to see visual motion. Similarly damage to specific afferent nerve fibers results in a complete inability to sense the positions of one's limbs (p. 41). The precise pattern of interactions between neurons determines the character of mental events: Changes in the relative activity of different neurons alter perception of sensory attributes such as color, taste, and body orientation. So it is clear that an appreciation of perception at the level of neural activity is absolutely essential if you are to understand how we perceive the world.

However, a description of neural events underpinning perception is inadequate by itself because it cannot reveal their purpose. Another level of description is also required, which specifies the function role of the neural structures comprising the sensory systems. Functional descriptions frequently make use of functional block diagrams that specify the component parts of the system and how they relate to each other (see Chapter 5). Such diagrams are quite abstract descriptions; they are not designed to capture details of the neural substrate, such as how close together the neurons are in the nervous system. Indeed functional block diagrams make no commitment to the physical instantiation of the system. The aim is to capture what the system does, not how it is made.

All the sensory systems process information that they acquire from the outside world. Functional descriptions tell us what information is processed, and how. There is yet a third level of description at a more abstract level than functional descriptions, which offers insight as to why those particular functions are needed for perception. This level is concerned with the fundamental computational goals of the system, and the constraints within which it operates. The description at this level may involve fundamental mathematical or computational properties that would constrain any system that attempts to interpret incoming sensory data, regardless of specific implementations.

This tripartite division into three levels of description – neural, functional, and computational – was proposed by Marr (1982) in the context of vision, but it can be applied across all the sensory systems. A complete understanding of each system requires a consideration of all three levels, and previous chapters have introduced the basic concepts that apply at each level. Let's take a specific example, and see how it can be understood at all three levels: adaptation. It has been widely observed at the neural level; individual sensory neurons show a reduction in responsiveness following prolonged exposure to stimulation (see p. 69). At the functional level adaptation has far-reaching consequences for perception because it alters the appearance of stimuli; stationary patterns appear to move, odors seem to disappear; sounds become quieter (see p. 66). At the computational level, the goal of adaptation is to minimize redundancy and maximize signal efficiency; adaptation serves to remove signals that are uninformative and wasteful because they are unchanging. If one omitted consideration of any one of the three levels of description, our understanding of adaptation would be incomplete. The links between the three levels are fairly loose, but they are important. Adaptation is just one possible way to satisfy the computational goal of reducing redundancy, for instance, and it can be implemented in many different neural processes (depletion of cell resources, inhibitory interactions between cells).

Specialization

When the functional properties of the sensory systems are examined in detail a common theme emerges across the senses: specialization of function. Individual neurons are specialized in the sense that each responds only to a specific set of sensory stimuli, whether sound frequencies, light wavelengths, or chemical compounds (p. 43). On a larger scale, whole cortical areas specialize in specific sensory modalities (p. 33).

As Figure 10.1 illustrates, all the sensory information you receive about the world comes from just four different kinds of specialized receptor (mechanoreceptors, chemoreceptors, photoreceptors, nociceptors). Sensory receptors mediate six distinct sensory modalities by virtue of the different brain regions where the signals arrive (vision, hearing, touch/pain, balance, smell, taste). Within each modality information is often broken down into submodalities served by specialized secondary brain areas. In vision and hearing, processing divides into two separate streams of cortical processing, perhaps carrying information about where objects are in the world, and what they are. Higher order cortical areas integrate information across the different sensory modalities.

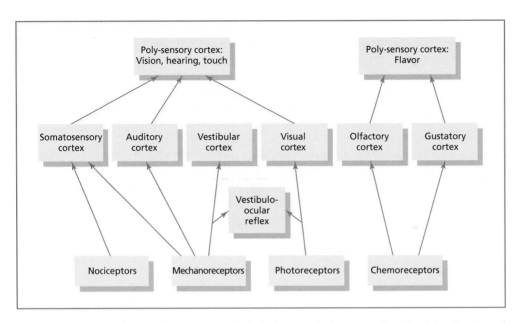

Figure 10.1 Some salient features of sensory processing in the human central nervous system. Signals from four types of receptor travel along seven different pathways to reach six distinct cortical areas. Higher level cortical areas integrate information across the sensory modalities.

Psychophysical studies reveal that functional specialization has many significant consequences for perception across all the sensory systems, from selective adaptation to dramatic variations in sensitivity to different stimuli within a modality (vision is much sharper near the center of fixation; touch is much more acute at the fingertips).

Ambiguity

Empirical data and theoretical analysis show that sensory processing is plagued by ambiguity, which takes two general forms, neural ambiguity and stimulus ambiguity.

Neural ambiguity

The responses of individual neurons are ambiguous because of the problem of univariance (p. 92). Each neuron is sensitive to several stimulus dimensions, but its response can vary only along one dimension. The brain resolves neural ambiguity by comparing responses across populations of neurons.

Stimulus ambiguity

Regardless of the limitations imposed by neural responses, the sensory systems must deal with a more fundamental ambiguity because of the inherent limitations of sensory data. Incoming information usually reflects a complex interaction between a number of environmental variables. In the case of vision and hearing, for example, these include the objects present, their layout, the position of the recipient, the nature of the light source (for vision), the reverberant properties of the surfaces present (for hearing), and so on (see Figure 7.1, p. 110). The task facing each of the sensory systems is to disentangle these factors in order to isolate the most important ones relating to the objects present and their layout. Mathematical analyses have revealed that there is usually insufficient information in the incoming data to solve the problem definitively: sensory stimuli are inherently ambiguous. Current theories of perception propose that the ambiguity is resolved by invoking additional information sources, based on prior knowledge of the structure of the sensory environment.

Resolving ambiguity

The pervasive nature of ambiguity means that perception is above all an inferential process in which decisions are based on incomplete sensory information; constrained guessing. Population codes are pivotal. On the one hand they solve the problem of neural ambiguity. On the other hand they supply the data for processes of perceptual inference that combine prior knowledge with current sensory input. Bayesian inference has become the dominant theoretical framework for resolving stimulus ambiguity across all the sensory systems.

Representation

When you see, hear, or feel something those experiences can be traced to tiny electrical currents circulating in complex, specialized brain circuits spanning billions of cortical neurons. These signals constitute internal representations of the world that you carry round in your head. They are, in effect, models of the outside world through which you capture important properties and which allow you to interact with the world and anticipate future events. Representations are built up in a series of processing stages (p. 83), starting with relatively simple representations of primitive stimulus properties such as visual orientation or sound frequency, and ending with sophisticated, abstract representations of objects and their properties.

Future directions

Any scientist working on sensation and perception will tell you that we do not yet know all the answers. As in any branch of science, each new experiment answers some questions, but inevitably raises others. Progress involves an incremental accumulation of empirical knowledge and theoretical understanding. So there are always new discoveries to be made, for instance about the specific forms taken by interactions between the sensory modalities, or about the detailed computations through which we judge the pitch of a sound or the speed of a moving visual object. In this section I will step back from issues of detail and attempt to identify some broad directions that are likely to feature in future research on perception. It is inevitably rather speculative and personal, but may give you a flavor of some of the major unresolved issues. It is subdivided into scientific issues and applications.

Scientific issues

Bottom-up and top-down processing

In the latter half of the twentieth century there was an increasing appreciation of the difficulties involved in trying to make meaningful interpretations of incoming sensory data. As mentioned in the previous section, ambiguity is a major problem. Significant progress has been made in our understanding of how the sensory systems resolve ambiguity. The solution involves both bottom-up information and top-down information flows. However, our understanding of the interplay between these two processing routes is far from complete, and efforts to increase understanding in this area are likely to be a major focus for future research. Bayesian inference is a powerful computational theory, but we need to know a great deal more about how it is implemented in the brain, what assumptions or 'priors' are used, and why (see Kersten *et al.*, 2004).

Two streams of processing

As you have read in earlier chapters, a lot of evidence has accumulated which indicates that sensory processing divides into two streams of processing, often called the ventral stream and the dorsal stream (p. 35). However there is no universal agreement on the best way to characterize the different functional roles of the two streams. One characterization distinguishes between 'what' and 'where' processing, while another distinguishes between 'conscious perception' and 'unconscious action'. Future research that resolves this issue will have a major impact on how we view the working of the human sensory systems. It is also possible that the distinction will fade in significance, as discoveries accumulate to show that the two streams are intimately linked and not nearly as distinctive as was first thought (see Farivar, 2009).

Natural stimuli

Historically the bulk of research on sensation and perception has used highly artificial stimuli, such as simple visual grating patterns or pure tones (pp. 62 and 95), for very sound methodological reasons. Such stimuli allow precise control of all relevant stimulus parameters, and ensure reproducibility by other researchers. However, there is an increasing and very promising trend toward using more natural stimuli in experimental research, and this trend is likely to increase for two reasons. First, it is increasingly possible to predict sensory responses to complex stimuli on the basis of our detailed knowledge of simple stimuli, and this opens up new avenues of research to test those predictions. Second, new research is expanding our knowledge of the statistical properties of large collections of natural stimuli, which prompts new questions about whether and how the sensory systems exploit these statistical properties. Research based on natural stimuli may also reveal aspects of the sensory systems that have been overlooked in research using simple artificial stimuli. For example: single cell studies using natural stimuli have shown that cortical neurons change their tuning adaptively to increase the amount of information carried by their response (Sharpee et al., 2006); illusions of apparent visual length may relate to the statistical properties of natural images (Howe & Purves, 2002).

Consciousness

The ultimate challenge for research on sensation and perception is to explain conscious perception. As you saw in the previous chapter, quite a lot is known about which aspects of neural activity are correlated with particular perceptual experiences. There is no general agreement on whether conscious experience is a by-product of neural processing or a causal element. Indeed there is no general agreement on the best ways to measure consciousness in an experiment. Nor do we know how neural activity produces consciousness. There are currently no answers within sight for these really fundamental questions about conscious perception; it is not even clear what kind of answer to look for. Here is a clear challenge for future research.

Future applications of perceptual science

As knowledge of human sensation and perception accumulates, the opportunities to apply that knowledge multiply. In some cases, such as sensory substitution, applications are quite tightly coupled to knowledge about how the human systems work. In other cases, such as machine perception, the application does not have to use methods that mimic the human sensory system, but as the most successful system in existence it offers valuable pointers to the best way forward.

Machine perception

A severe test of the current level of understanding in perception is to build a machine capable of perceiving the world, at least in the sense that it can recognize objects or navigate through a cluttered environment. Potential applications are almost limitless, from automated control of manufacturing to medical diagnosis, surveillance, and exploration of hazardous environments. Simple forms of machine perception are already a part of everyday life. Many current digital cameras have built-in technology to detect human faces and focus on them; quality control in many industrial processes relies on automatic visual detection of imperfections. However, beyond these relatively simple applications machine perception still faces some stiff challenges. The problems stem from the complexity of the task. Humans can effortlessly use body characteristics such as the face and voice to recognize each other. Research on biometrics attempts to simulate this ability with a (preferably infallible) method for automatic identification on the basis of unique physical or behavioral traits. A number of traits have been studied, including the face, fingerprint, iris, retina, voice, and gait (Figure 10.2). The most successful technologies are based on fingerprints, iris scans, retina scans, and palm-prints (Jain et al., 2004).

No presently available automatic systems can match the ability of a typical human to recognize people or to drive a vehicle. The most successful automatic recognition systems incorporate powerful

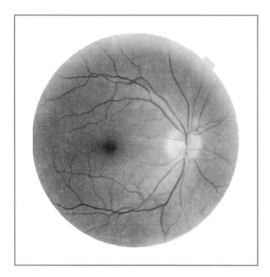

Figure 10.2 The pattern of blood vessels in the author's retina, which is a unique, stable biometric marker of identity. Retinal scanning is fast but relatively intrusive, since the scanner must be placed quite close to the eye.

constraints that improve performance but limit their application to very specific situations. For example, 'electronic nose' devices have advanced considerably in recent years, and find numerous applications in, for example, the agricultural, biomedical, food, and cosmetics industries. However the most successful applications use a small number of sensors designed specifically for those applications (Wilson & Baietto, 2009).

Sensory substitution

Recent advances in our knowledge of plasticity in the human sensory systems (p. 51), coupled with advances in instrumentation technology, offer opportunities for sensory substitution. In a sensory substitution device a sensory loss to one system (e.g. sight) can be compensated by substituting it with information from an artificial receptor, usually supplied to an intact sense organ. For instance, the traditional approach for a blind person is to use touch to read specially created tactile text (Braille), but recent advances allow real-time presentation of information about complex visual scenes. A blind person can be trained to recognize visual patterns using tactile stimulation delivered by a device placed on the tongue (Kupers *et al.*, 2006). Another device for blind people uses sound; height in the visual field is conveyed by pitch, and brightness by loudness in a left-to-right scan of the scene (Ward & Meijer, 2010). Wearers of this device report that they do perceive something akin to a visual experience rather than an auditory one.

Future work on sensory substitution devices offers the prospect of dramatic improvements in the quality of life for those wearing them, and may also shed new light on hitherto unknown capacities of the human sensory systems.

Evaluation

By and large the major anatomical structures and functional properties of the human sensory systems are now well established in the scientific literature, though there are, as always, matters of detail still to be resolved (e.g. some aspects of chemoreception remain mysterious). Arguably we know more about the physiology of the sensory pathways, and about the basic psychophysics of sensory perception, than about any other aspect of the human nervous system. The major challenges for future research appear to reside at higher levels of processing where perceptual inferences are drawn, information is merged between the senses, and information is shared with other cognitive processes such as attention and memory.

Insights into the problem of ambiguity in perception initially came from attempts to build machines that can perceive the world. At the start of this enterprise in the mid-1950s, researchers expected to solve the major problems within 10 to 20 years (Crevier, 1993). The problems facing researchers in machine intelligence were much more severe than many had anticipated, and there are still no machines capable of doing anything but the simplest perceptual tasks. Nevertheless the problems gave an insight into the formidable power of human sensory processes. Future work on the application of perceptual science to machine perception and to sensory substitution offers the prospect of new insights into the workings of the perceiving brain, as well as substantial benefits for society.

Summary

- A tripartite division into three essential levels of description and understanding (neural, functional, computational) applies equally well across all the human sensory systems.
- Ambiguity is pervasive in sensation and perception, and population codes carried by specialized groups of neurons are pivotal in its resolution.
- Modern theories of perception are theories about how the brain constructs internal representations of the world.
- Major scientific issues remain to be resolved concerning the interplay between different processing routes (bottom-up/top-down, ventral/dorsal), the use of more natural stimuli, and the origin of conscious perceptual experience.
- Future applications of perceptual science to machine perception and sensory substitution present severe tests of our knowledge and offer the prospect of new insights into the workings of the perceiving brain.

REFLECTIVE EXERCISE

1. Ambiguity in perceptual processing is caused by:
   a. Two streams of processing
   b. Univariance
   c. Population codes
   d. Bayesian inference

2. Use two examples from different sensory systems to illustrate the importance of all three levels of description in perception (neural, functional, computational).

3. Evaluate the benefits to society that may accrue from applying current knowledge about the workings of the sensory systems.

FURTHER READING

- Bach-y-Rita, P., & Kercel, S.W. (2003) Sensory substitution and the human–machine interface. *Trends in Cognitive Sciences, 7,* 541–546.
- Crevier, D. (1993) *AI: The Tumultuous History of the Search for Artificial Intelligence*. New York: HarperCollins.
- Farivar, R. (2009) Dorsal–ventral integration in object recognition. *Brain Research Reviews, 61,* 144–153.
- Motoyoshi, I., Nishida, S., Sharan, L., & Adelson, E.H. (2007) Image statistics and the perception of surface qualities. *Nature, 447,* 206–209.
- Wilson, A.D., & Baietto, M. (2009) Applications and advances in electronic-nose technologies. *Sensors, 9,* 5099–5148.

Glossary

Achromatopsia. A clinical disorder in which the patient is unable to perceive color, usually because of damage to an area of secondary visual cortex called V4.

Agnosia. A clinical disorder in which the patient is unable to visually perceive shapes or objects.

Akinetopsia. A rare neurological disorder also known as 'motion blindness', in which the patient cannot perceive visual movement despite being able to recognize and locate objects visually; usually caused by damage to an area of secondary visual cortex called MT.

Amacrine cell. A class of retinal cell whose axons spread laterally in deeper retinal layers, making contact with many bipolar and ganglion cells.

Analog representation. A representational system in which continuously variable magnitudes in one physical system signify corresponding magnitudes in another system.

Apperceptive agnosia. A clinical visual disorder involving an inability to name, copy, or match even simple shapes.

Asomatognosia. A clinical disorder in which the patient fails to recognize their own limbs on one side of the body, following damage in the right-hand cerebral cortex.

Associative agnosia. A clinical visual disorder in which objects cannot be recognized from their shapes, even though they can be copied and matched with little difficulty.

Basilar membrane. A flexible partition running along the length of the cochlea, which houses the mechanoreceptors that transduce sound energy into electrical signals.

Bayes' theorem. A mathematical formula for drawing inferences by combining different sources of evidence, such as current information and past experience.

Bayesian inference. An inference drawn by combining different sources of evidence according to a rigorous mathematical formula; see Chapter 7.

Bipolar cell. A class of retinal cell that conveys responses from the photoreceptors to retinal ganglion cells. Different subtypes carry responses from rods and from cones.

Bottom-up processing. A processing scheme in which information flows up from lower levels to higher levels of analysis, integrating simple sensory attributes into large structures on the basis of built-in rules.

Cartesian dualism. A philosophical tradition named after René Descartes, which posits that mind and brain are fundamentally different in kind; one cannot be reduced to the other.

Cerebellar cortex. A large, complex structure thought to be crucial for the unconscious control of movement, posture, and balance.

Cerebral cortex. A thin, densely folded sheet of neurons covering the brain; although it is only 3 mm thick, the cerebral cortex has a total surface area of over two square meters, and contains about 10 billion brain cells.

Cochlea. A spiral-shaped organ in the inner ear, where sound vibrations are transduced into electrical signals.

Computational neuroscience. A modern discipline that attempts to understand brain function by analyzing and simulating the computations that it performs.

Cone. A type of photoreceptor that is specialized for responding in bright illumination.

Connectionist. A theoretical approach in computational neuroscience based on large networks of interconnected simple processing units.

Cornea. The curved, transparent membrane through which light enters the eye.

Cortical magnification. Distortion of a sensory cortical map that reflects the number of receptors devoted to each part of the sensory surface.

Crista. A patch of sensory hair cells in a swelling (ampulla) of each semi-circular canal.

Epiphenomenalism. A theory which posits that consciousness is caused by neural activity, but has no causal influence on activity.

Fechner's Law. A principle describing the relationship between sensation magnitude and stimulus magnitude.

Fovea. A small area at the center of the retina, containing many densely packed cone photoreceptors but no rods.

Frontal lobe. One of the four lobes of the cerebral cortex, thought to be essential for planning and controlling behavior.

Gestalt psychology. A theoretical movement that emphasized perceptual grouping on the basis of a set of rules or laws such as similarity and proximity.

Horizontal cell. A class of retinal cell whose axons spread laterally, making contact with several photoreceptors.

Hue. Sensory impression of the color of a light or a surface, such as 'red', 'magenta', or 'green'.

Identity theory. A theory that identifies consciousness with neural activity in the brain; all conscious events must have corresponding neural events.

Information theory. A branch of mathematical theory concerned with the efficiency with which information can be transmitted through a processing system; see Chapter 5.

Just noticeable difference (JND). The smallest change in sensory stimulation that can be reliably detected by an experimental participant, measured using a psychophysical method.

Lens. A transparent object with a curved surface, which bends light passing through it to create an image on a suitably positioned surface placed behind it.

Likelihood. A probability value used in Bayesian inference, which estimates the probability of a particular interpretation on the basis of current sensory information.

Maximum posterior probability (MAP). A rule for selecting among alternative interpretations, based on comparing their posterior probabilities and selecting the maximum among them.

Mechanoreceptor. A class of sensory receptor cell that responds to mechanical distortion or deflection, such as a hair cell in the ear.

Mental causation. A theory which posits that intentional mental states cause intentional actions.

Metamer. Two colors or lights that appear the same hue but contain different light wavelengths.

Mitral cell. A neuron in the olfactory bulb that receives signals from olfactory receptor cells and relays them to the brain.

Motion after-effect (MAE). Following adaptation to visual movement in a particular direction, a stationary pattern appears to move in the opposite direction.

Multi-sensory neuron. A sensory neuron that responds to stimulation in at least two modalities, such as vision and audition.

Nervous system. The complex network of nerve cells that controls all bodily functions; the *central nervous system* (CNS) comprises the brain and spinal cord; the *peripheral nervous system* lies outside the brain and spinal cord, and includes sensory neurons, motor neurons, and their nerve fibers.

Neural correlate of consciousness (NCC). The set of neural events that give rise to a specific conscious experience

Nociceptor. A class of sensory receptor that has no specialized nerve ending, but responds to dangerously intense stimuli associated with pain sensations.

Noise. Information in a transmission system that is unrelated to the signal, and serves to make the signal more difficult to decipher.

Occipital lobe. One of the four lobes of the cerebral cortex, known to be devoted to sensory processing of visual information.

Olfactory bulb. A mass of neurons projecting from the brain behind the nose, which contains the mitral cells that carry olfactory responses.

Pacinian corpuscle. A type of sensory receptor that is sensitive to mechanical distortion; see Figure 1.2.

Parietal lobe. One of the four lobes of the cerebral cortex, thought to be important for guiding selective attention to stimuli.

Perception. A complex, meaningful experience of an external event or object, created from a combination of many different sensations.

Placebo effect. A measurable physiological or behavioral response produced by administration of an inert or 'dummy' substance or procedure.

Point of subjective equality (PSE). The 50% point of a psychometric function, at which the participant is equally disposed toward two alternative responses.

Population code. A processing scheme in which different values of a stimulus attribute such as color or tilt are coded by different patterns of activity in a population of neurons.

Posterior probability. The probability that a particular interpretation is correct, based on combining prior and likelihood values for that interpretation.

Prior. A probability value used in Bayesian inference, which estimates the probability of a particular interpretation on the basis of prior information (experience).

Probability summation. A statistical effect in which the detection rate of a signal improves as the number of opportunities to detect it increases.

Prosopagnosia. A clinical disorder in which the patient is unable to recognize faces.

Psychophysics. The scientific study of the relation between physical stimulation and perceptual experience.

Pupil. The circular aperture lying between the cornea and the lens, which regulates the amount of light entering the eye.

Qualia. Primitive conscious mental states, such as the felt quality of a color or a sound.

Receptive field. The area of a receptive surface such as the skin or the retina in which stimulation causes a sensory neuron to respond.

Redundancy. A term used to describe signal components that add little, if anything, to the information content of a signal.

Retina. A network of cells lining the inside of the eye, containing the photoreceptors that transduce light energy into electrical signals.

Retinal ganglion cell. A class of retinal cell whose fibers form the optic nerve, carrying the output signal from the retina.

Rod. A type of photoreceptor that is specialized for responding in dim illumination.

Saccule and **utricle.** Two chambers in the vestibular organ which contain receptors that signal head tilt and linear acceleration.

Scotoma. A small area of blindness in the field of view, caused by damage to the visual pathway or cortex.

Semi-circular canals. Three ring-shaped canals in each vestibular organ, arranged approximately at right-angles to each other; they contain receptors that signal angular acceleration of the head.

Sensation. An elementary experience evoked by stimulation of a sense organ, such as brightness, loudness, or saltiness.

Sensorineural hearing loss. Permanent deafness caused by damage to cochlear hair cells.

Sensory map. An ordered, topographical arrangement of sensory neurons that reflects the structure of the relevant sensory surface (the body, the retina, the cochlea).

Sensory receptor. A specialized nerve cell that transduces environmental energy into an electrical signal.

Sparse code. An efficient form of population coding characterized by strong activity in only a small subset of the neural population; it can be achieved using inhibitory interactions between the neurons.

Spatial frequency. Standard measure of the fineness of the bars in a grating pattern, which corresponds to the number of dark–light cycles per unit of visual angle (per degree).

Spectral reflectance. The proportion of incident light reflected from a surface at different wavelengths in the spectrum.

Subliminal stimulus. A sensory stimulus that is too weak to be consciously perceived but may nevertheless influence perception, cognition, or action.

Superior colliculus. A mass of neurons in the midbrain that is thought to be involved in integrating visual and auditory signals, and in directing visual attention.

Symbolic representation. A representational system in which abstract, discrete symbols in one physical system signify discrete entities or states in another system.

Synapse. A junction between two neurons where chemical signals pass from one neuron to the other.

Temporal frequency. Standard measure of flicker rate in a visual stimulus, which corresponds to the number of on–off cycles per second, measured in hertz (Hz).

Top-down processing. A processing scheme in which information flows down from higher levels to lower levels of analysis, using prior knowledge and experience to steer lower level processes.

Transduction. The conversion of environmental energy into neural signals by sensory receptor cells.

Trichromacy theory. The theory that color appearance can be explained by the pattern of responses across the three types of cone receptor in the human retina.

Univariance. A computational problem in sensory coding arising from the fact that the response of a sensory neuron usually depends on several stimulus dimensions, but can only vary along one dimension.

Vestibulo-ocular reflexes. Reflex circuits that include vestibular receptors and eye muscles, which control eye movements that compensate for head movements to maintain a stable retinal image.

Vestibular labyrinths/organs. Bony, fluid-filled structures buried deep in the temporal bone of the head, which house the receptors that signal head position and movement.

Visual angle. A unit of measurement specifying how large the image of an object is at the retina, based on the angle it subtends; see Figure 1.7.

Visual field. The entire area of space that can be seen from the eye without changing its position.

Weber fraction. The constant fractional value associated with a JND.

Weber's Law. The principle that the JND is a constant fraction of the initial stimulus value.

References

Adrian, E.D., & Zotterman, Y. (1926) The impulses produced by sensory nerve-endings. Part 2. The response of a single end-organ. *Journal of Physiology, 61*, 151–171.

Alais, D., & Burr, D. (2004) The ventriloquist effect results from near-optimal bimodal integration. *Current Biology, 14*, 257–262.

Alvarado, J.C., Vaughan, J.W., Stanford, T.R., & Stein, B.E. (2007) Multisensory versus unisensory integration: contrasting modes in the superior colliculus. *Journal of Neurophysiology, 97*, 3193–3205.

Anstis, S. (1998) Picturing peripheral acuity. *Perception, 27*, 817–825.

Barlow, H.B. (1953) Summation and inhibition in the frog's retina. *Journal of Physiology, 119*, 69–88.

Barlow, H.B. (1972) Single units and sensation: a neuron doctrine for perceptual psychology? *Perception, 1*, 371–394.

Baron-Cohen, S., Harrison, J., Goldstein, L.H., & Wyke, M. (1993) Coloured speech perception: is synaesthesia what happens when modularity breaks down? *Perception, 22*, 419–426.

Baron-Cohen, S., Burt, L., Smith-Laittan, F., Harrison, J., & Bolton, P. (1996) Synaesthesia: prevalence and familiality. *Perception, 25*, 1073–1079.

Baylor, D.A. (1987) Photoreceptor signals and vision. *Investigative Ophthalmology and Visual Science, 28*, 34–49.

Beauchamp, G.K. (2009) Sensory and receptor responses to umami: an overview of pioneering work. *American Journal of Clinical Nutrition, 90* (Suppl), 723S–727S.

Beauchamp, G.K., & Moran, M.M. (1982) Dietary experience and sweet taste preference in human infants. *Appetite, 3*, 139–152.

Bermeitinger, C., Goelz, R., Johr, N., Neumann, M., Ecker, U.K.H., & Doerr, R. (2009) The hidden persuaders break into the tired brain. *Journal of Experimental Social Psychology, 45*, 320–326.

Blake, R., & Hiris, E. (1993) Another means for measuring the motion aftereffect. *Vision Research, 33*, 1589–1592.

Blakemore, C., Carpenter, R.H.S., & Georgeson, M.A. (1970) Lateral inhibition between orientation detectors in the human visual system. *Nature, 228*, 37–39.

Blakemore, S.J., Wolpert, D.M., & Frith, C.D. (2000) Why can't you tickle yourself? *NeuroReport, 1*, R11–R16.

Bogen, J.E. (1995) On the neurophysiology of consciousness: I. An overview. *Consciousness and Cognition*, *4*, 52–62.

Bolanowski, S.J., & Zwislocki, J.J. (1984) Intensity and frequency characteristics of Pacinian corpuscles. I. Action potentials. *Journal of Neurophysiology*, *51*, 793–811.

Bradley, M.M., Miccoli, L., Escrig, A., & Lang, P.J. (2008) The pupil as a measure of emotional arousal and autonomic activation. *Psychophysiology*, *45*, 602–607.

Burr, D., & Ross, J. (1986) Visual processing of motion. *Trends in Neurosciences*, *9*, 304–307.

Calvert, G., Bullmore, E.T., Brammer, M.J., Campbell, R., Williams, S.C.R., McGuire, P.K., *et al.* (1997) Activation of auditory cortex during silent lipreading. *Science*, *276*, 593–596.

Calvin, W.H., & Ojemann, G.A. (1994) *Conversations with Neil's Brain: The Neural Nature of Thought and Language*. New York: Addison-Wesley.

Campbell, F.W., & Robson, J.G. (1968) Application of Fourier analysis to the visibility of gratings. *Journal of Physiology*, *197*, 551–556.

Carroll, G. (Producer), & Scott, R. (Director) (1979) *Alien* [Motion Picture]. United States: 20th Century Fox.

Carter, O., Konkle, T., Wang, Q., Hayward, V., & Moore, C. (2008) Tactile rivalry demonstrated with an ambiguous apparent-motion quartet. *Current Biology*, *18*, 1050–1054.

Castiello, U., & Jeannerod, M. (1991) Measuring time to awareness. *NeuroReport*, *2*, 797–800.

Cole, J. (1998) Rehabilitation after sensory neuronopathy syndrome. *Journal of the Royal Society of Medicine*, *91*, 30–32.

Crevier, D. (1993) *AI: The Tumultuous History of the Search for Artificial Intelligence*. New York: HarperCollins.

Crick, F., & Koch, C. (2003) A framework for consciousness. *Nature Neuroscience*, *6*, 119–126.

Critchley, H.D., & Rolls, E.T. (1996) Hunger and satiety modify the responses of olfactory and visual neurons in the primate orbitofrontal cortex. *Journal of Neurophysiology*, *75*, 1673–1686.

Dartnall, H.J.A., Bowmaker, J.K., & Mollon, J.D. (1983) Human visual pigments: microspectrophotometric results from the eyes of seven persons. *Proceedings of the Royal Society of London, Series B*, *220*, 115–130.

de Lange, H. (1958) Research into the dynamic nature of the human fovea–cortex systems with intermittent and modulated light. I. Attenuation characteristics with white and colored light. *Journal of the Optical Society of America*, *48*, 777–784.

De Valois, R., Albrecht, D., & Thorell, L. (1982) Spatial frequency selectivity of cells in macaque visual cortex. *Vision Research*, *22*, 545–559.

Drewing, K., & Ernst, M.O. (2006) Integration of force and position cues for shape perception through active touch. *Brain Research*, *1078*, 92–100.

Driver, J., & Noesselt, T. (2008) Multisensory interplay reveals crossmodal influences on 'sensory-specific' brain regions, neural responses, and judgements. *Neuron, 57*, 11–23.

Eastman, N., & Campbell, C. (2006) Neuroscience and legal determination of criminal responsibility. *Nature Reviews Neuroscience, 7*, 311–318.

Ernst, M.O., & Banks, M.S. (2002) Humans integrate visual and haptic information in a statistically optimal fashion. *Nature, 415*, 429–433.

Ernst, M.O., & Bulthoff, H.H. (2004) Merging the senses into a robust percept. *Trends in Cognitive Sciences, 8*, 162–169.

Falchier, A., Clavagnier, S., Barone, P., & Kennedy, H. (2002) Anatomical evidence of multimodal integration in primate striate cortex. *Journal of Neuroscience, 22*, 5749–5759.

Fang, F., Kersten, D., & Murray, S.O. (2008) Perceptual grouping and inverse fMRI activity patterns in human visual cortex. *Journal of Vision, 8*, 2–9.

Farah, M.J. (2004) *Visual Agnosia*. Second Edition. Cambridge, MA: MIT Press.

Farivar, R. (2009) Dorsal–ventral integration in object recognition. *Brain Research Reviews, 61*, 144–153.

Feinberg, T.E., Venneri, A., Simone, A.M., Fan, Y., & Northoff, G. (2010) The neuroanatomy of asomatognosia and somatoparaphrenia. *Journal of Neurology, Neurosurgery, and Psychiatry, 81*, 276–281.

Feynman, R. (1998) *Six Easy Pieces: Fundamentals of Physics Explained*. London: Penguin.

Finlay, D., Dodwell, P., & Caelli, T. (1984) The waggon-wheel effect. *Perception, 13*, 237–248.

Firestein, S. (2001) How the olfactory system makes sense of scents. *Nature, 413*, 211–218.

Fitzpatrick, D.C., Batra, R., Stanford, T.R., & Kuwada, S. (1997) A neuronal population code for sound localization. *Nature, 388*, 871–874.

Frisby, J.P., & Stone, J.V. (2010) *Seeing: The Computational Approach to Biological Vision*. Cambridge, MA: MIT Press.

Frith, C.D., & Frith, U. (2007) Social cognition in humans. *Current Biology, 17*, R724–R732.

Garstang, M. (2004) Long-distance, low-frequency elephant communication. *Journal of Comparative Physiology A, 190*, 791–805.

Gegenfurtner, K.R., Mayser, H., & Sharpe, L.T. (1999) Seeing movement in the dark. *Nature, 398*, 475–476.

Gibson, J.J. (1950) *The Perception of the Visual World*. Boston, MA: Houghton Mifflin.

Glickstein, M., & Whitteridge, D. (1987). Tatsuji Inouye and the mapping of the visual fields on the human cerebral cortex. *Trends in Neurosciences, 10*, 350–353.

Goodale, M.A., & Milner, A.D. (1992) Separate visual pathways for perception and action. *Trends in Neurosciences, 15*, 20–25.

Gould, S.J. (1997) The exaptive excellence of spandrels as a term and prototype. *Proceedings of the National Academy of Sciences USA, 94,* 10750–10755.

Gould, S.J., & Lewontin, R.C. (1979) The spandrels of San Marco and the Panglossian paradigm: a critique of the adaptionist programme. *Proceedings of the Royal Society, B, 205,* 581–598.

Graybiel, A., & Hupp, E.D. (1946) The oculogyral illusion: a form of apparent motion which may be observed following stimulation of the semi-circular canals. *Journal of Aviation Medicine, 17,* 3–27.

Green, D.M., & Swets, J.A. (1966) *Signal Detection Theory and Psychophysics.* Chichester, UK: Wiley.

Greene, J., & Cohen, J. (2004) For the law, neuroscience changes nothing and everything. *Philosophical Transactions of the Royal Society, B, 359,* 1775–1785.

Greenwald, A.G., Spangenberg, E.R., Pratkanis, A.R., & Eskenazi, J. (1991) Double-blind tests of subliminal self-help audiotapes. *Psychological Science, 2,* 119–122.

Gregory, R.L. (1997) Visual illusions classified. *Trends in Cognitive Sciences, 1,* 190–194.

Gross, C.G. (2002) Genealogy of the 'Grandmother Cell'. *Neuroscientist, 8,* 512–518.

Gurney, K. (2007) Neural networks for perceptual processing: from simulation tools to theories. *Philosophical Transactions of the Royal Society, Series B, 362,* 339–353.

Hammett, S.T., Champion, R.A., Thompson, P.G., & Morland, A.B. (2007) Perceptual distortions of speed at low luminance: evidence inconsistent with a Bayesian account of speed encoding. *Vision Research, 47*(4), 564–568.

Hammond, P., Mouat, G.S.V., & Smith, A.T. (1985) Motion after-effects in cat striate cortex elicited by moving gratings. *Experimental Brain Research, 60,* 411–416.

Helmholtz, H. von (1910) *Treatise on Physiological Optics Vol. III* (J.P.C. Southall ed.) (1962). New York: Dover.

Hillis, J.M., Watt, S.J., Landy, M.S., & Banks, M.S. (2004) Slant from texture and disparity cues: optimal cue combination. *Journal of Vision, 4,* 967–992.

Hofer, H., Carroll, J., Neitz, J., Neitz, M., & Williams, D.R. (2005) Organization of the human trichromatic cone mosaic. *Journal of Neuroscience, 25,* 9669–9679.

Howe, C.Q., & Purves, D. (2002) Range statistics can explain the anomalous perception of length. *Proceedings of the National Academy of Sciences, 99,* 13184–13188.

Hsieh, P.-J., Vul, E., & Kanwisher, N. (2010) Recognition alters the spatial pattern of fMRI activation in early retinotopic cortex. *Journal of Neurophysiology, 103,* 1501–1507.

Hubel, D., & Wiesel, T. (1959) Receptive fields of single neurones in the cat's striate cortex. *Journal of Physiology, 148,* 574–591.

Hubel, D., & Wiesel, T. (1977) Functional architecture of macaque monkey visual cortex. *Proceedings of the Royal Society of London, Series B, 198,* 1–59.

Hudspeth, A.J. (1989) How the ear's works work. *Nature, 341,* 397–404.

Jain, A.K., Ross, A., & Prabhakar, S. (2004) An introduction to biometric recognition. *IEEE Transactions on Circuits and Systems for Video Technology, 14,* 4–20.

Jaramillo, S., & Pearlmutter, B.A. (2006) Brightness illusions as optimal percepts. *Technical Report NUIM-CS-TR-2006-02,* Hamilton Institute, National University of Ireland Maynooth.

Jousmaki, V., & Hari, R. (1998) Parchment skin illusion: sound-biased touch. *Current Biology, 8,* R190.

Kaas, J.H., & Hackett, T.A. (2000) Subdivisions of auditory cortex and processing streams in primates. *Proceedings of the National Academy of Sciences USA, 97,* 11793–11799.

Karremans, J.C., Stroebe, W., & Claus, J. (2006) Beyond Vicary's fantasies: the impact of subliminal priming and brand choice. *Journal of Experimental Social Psychology, 42,* 792–798.

Kashino, M., & Nishida, S. (1998) Adaptation in the processing of interaural time differences revealed by the auditory localization aftereffect. *Journal of the Acoustical Society of America, 103,* 3597–3604.

Kayser, C., & Logothetis, N.K. (2007) Do early cortices integrate cross-modal information? *Brain Structure and Function, 212,* 121–132.

Kelly, D.H. (1966) Frequency doubling in visual responses. *Journal of the Optical Society of America, 11,* 1628–1633.

Kersten, D., Mamassian, P., & Yuille, A. (2004) Object perception as Bayesian inference. *Annual Review of Psychology, 55,* 271–304.

Kinney, H.C., Korein, J., Panigrahy, A., Dikkes, P., & Goode, R. (1994) Neuropathological findings in the brain of Karen Ann Quinlan. *New England Journal of Medicine, 330,* 1469–1475.

Kondo, H.M., & Kashino, M. (2007) Neural mechanisms of auditory awareness underlying verbal transformations. *NeuroImage, 36,* 123–130.

Krubitzer, L. (1995) The organization of the neocortex in mammals: are species differences really so different? *Trends in Neurosciences, 18,* 408–417.

Kuffler, S.W. (1953) Discharge patterns and functional organization of mammalian retina. *Journal of Neurophysiology, 16,* 37–68.

Kupers, R., Fumal, A., de Noordhout, A.M., Gjedde, A., Schoenen, J., & Ptito, M. (2006) Transcranial magnetic stimulation of the visual cortex induces somatotopically organised qualia in blind subjects. *Proceedings of the National Academy of Sciences USA, 103,* 13256–13260.

Lackner, J.R., & DiZio, P. (2006) Space motion sickness. *Experimental Brain Research, 175,* 377–399.

Lashley, K.S., Chow, K.-L., & Semmes, J. (1951) An examination of the electrical field theory of cerebral integration. *Psychological Review, 58,* 123–136.

Lee, T.S., & Mumford, D. (2003) Hierarchical Bayesian inference in the visual cortex. *Journal of the Optical Society of America A, 20,* 1434–1448.

Lennie, P. (2000) Color vision: putting it all together. *Current Biology, 10,* R589–R591.

Lennie, P. (2003) The cost of cortical computation. *Current Biology, 13,* 493–497.

Li, X., Li, W., Wang, H., Bayley, D.L., Cao, J., Reed, D.R., *et al.* (2006) Cats lack a sweet taste receptor. *Journal of Nutrition, 136,* 1932S–1934S.

Libet, B. (1985) Unconscious cerebral initiative and the role of conscious will in voluntary action. *Behavioral and Brain Sciences, 8,* 529–566.

Long, G.M., & Moran, C.J. (2007) How to keep a reversible figure from reversing: teasing out top-down and bottom-up processes. *Perception, 36,* 431–445.

Maia, T.V., & Cleeremans, A. (2005) Consciousness: converging insights from connectionist modeling and neuroscience. *Trends in Cognitive Sciences, 9,* 397–404.

Malnic, B., Hirono, J., Sato, T., & Buck, L.B. (1999) Combinatorial receptor codes for odors. *Cell, 96,* 713–723.

Manoussaki, D., Chadwick, R.S., Ketten, D.R., Arruda, J., Dimitriadis, E.K., & O'Malley, J.T. (2008) The influence of cochlear shape on low-frequency hearing. *Proceedings of the National Academy of Sciences, 105,* 6162–6166.

Marr, D. (1982) *Vision.* New York: Freeman.

Martin, G.N. (2004) A neuroanatomy of flavour. *Petits Propos Culinaires (PPC), 76,* 58–82.

Mather, G. (2009) *Foundations of Sensation and Perception.* Second Edition. Hove, UK: Psychology Press.

Mather, G., Verstraten, F., & Anstis, S. (eds) (1998) *The Motion Aftereffect: A Modern Perspective.* Cambridge, MA: MIT Press.

McGinn, C. (1993) *The Problem of Consciousness.* Malden, MA: Blackwell.

McGurk, H., & MacDonald, T. (1976) Hearing lips and seeing voices. *Nature, 264,* 746–748.

Micheyl, C., Carlyon, R.P., Gutschalk, A., Melcher, J.R., Oxenham, A.J., Rauschecker, J.P., *et al.* (2007) The role of auditory cortex in the formation of auditory streams. *Hearing Research, 229,* 116–131.

Money, K.E., & Miles, W.S. (1974) Heavy water nystagmus and effects of alcohol. *Nature, 247,* 404–405.

Mooney, C. (1957) Age in the development of closure ability in children. *Canadian Journal of Psychology, 11,* 219–226

Moore, B.C.J. (1997) *An Introduction to the Psychology of Hearing.* San Diego, CA: Academic Press.

Morgan, M.J. (1980) Analogue models of motion perception. *Philosophical Transactions of the Royal Society of London, B, 290,* 117–135.

Morgan, M.J. (1996) Visual illusions. In V. Bruce (ed.) *Unsolved Mysteries of the Mind* (pp. 29–58). Hove, UK: Lawrence Erlbaum Associates Ltd.

Morrell, C.H., Gordon-Salant, S., Pearson, J.D., Brant, L.J., & Fozard, J.L. (1996) Age- and gender-specific reference ranges for hearing level and longitudinal changes in hearing level. *Journal of the Acoustical Society of America*, *100*, 1949–1967.

Mountcastle, V. (1957) Modality and topographic properties of single neurons of cat's somatic sensory cortex. *Journal of Neurophysiology*, *20*, 408–434.

Nagasako, E.M., Oaklander, A.L., & Dworkin, R.H. (2003) Congenital insensitivity to pain: an update. *Pain*, *101*, 213–219.

Naka, K.I., & Rushton, W.A.H. (1966) S-potentials from colour units in the retina of fish (*Cyprinidae*). *Journal of Physiology*, *185*, 536–555.

Neuweiler, G. (1984) Foraging, echolocation and audition in bats. *Naturwissenschaften*, *71*, 446–455.

Newell, A., & Simon, H.A. (1961) Computer simulation of human thinking. *Science*, *134*, 2011–2017.

Nunn, J.A., Gregory, L.J., Brammer, M., Williams, S.C.R., Parslow, D.M., Morgan, M.J., *et al.* (2002) Functional magnetic resonance imaging of synesthesia: activation of V4/V8 by spoken words. *Nature Neuroscience*, *5*, 371–375.

O'Doherty, J., Rolls, E.T., Francis, S., Bowtell, R., McGlone, F., Kobal, G., *et al.* (2000) Sensory-specific satiety-related olfactory activation of the human orbitofrontal cortex. *NeuroReport*, *11*, 893–897.

Palmer, A.R. (1995) Neural signal processing. In B.C.J. Moore (ed.) *Hearing*. San Diego, CA: Academic Press.

Parnes, L.S., Agrawal, S.K., & Atlas, J. (2003) Diagnosis and management of benign paroxysmal positional vertigo (BPPV). *Canadian Medical Association Journal*, *169*, 681–693.

Penfield, W. (1958) *The Excitable Cortex in Conscious Man*. Liverpool, UK: Liverpool University Press.

Penfield, W., & Rasmussen, T. (1950). *The Cerebral Cortex of Man: A Clinical Study of Localization of Function*. New York: Macmillan.

Pirenne, M. (1962) Dark-adaptation and night vision. In H. Davson (ed.) *The Eye* (Vol. 2, pp. 93–122). New York: Academic Press.

Plaut, D.C., & McClelland, J.L. (2010) Locating object knowledge in the brain: comment on Bowers's (2009) attempt to revive the Grandmother cell hypothesis. *Psychological Review*, *117*, 284–290.

Pouget, A., Dayan, P., & Zemel, R. (2000) Information processing with population codes. *Nature Reviews Neuroscience*, *1*, 125–132.

Quiroga, R.Q., Kreiman, G., Koch, C., & Fried, I. (2007) Sparse but not 'Grandmother-cell' coding in the medial temporal lobe. *Trends in Cognitive Sciences*, *12*, 87–91.

Ramachandran, V.S., & Hirstein, W. (1998) The perception of phantom limbs: the D.O. Hebb lecture. *Brain*, *121*, 1603–1630.

Rock, I., & Palmer, S. (1990) The legacy of Gestalt Psychology. *Scientific American*, *263*(6), 48–61.

Rolls, B.J., Rowe, E.A., & Rolls, E.T. (1982) How sensory properties of foods affect human feeding behaviour. *Physiology and Behavior*, *29*, 409–417.

Rolls, E.T. (2006) Brain mechanisms underlying flavour and appetite. *Philosophical Transactions of the Royal Society, B*, *361*, 1123–1136.

Ross, H.E., & Brodie, E.E. (1987) Weber fractions for weight and mass as a function of stimulus intensity. *Quarterly Journal of Experimental Psychology, Section A*, *39*, 77–88.

Roth, S., & Black, M.J. (2007) On the spatial statistics of optical flow. *International Journal of Computer Vision*, *74*, 33–50.

Rushton, W.A.H. (1961) Rhodopsin measurement and dark-adaptation in a subject deficient in cone vision. *Journal of Physiology*, *156*, 193–205.

Sack, A.T., Kohler, A., Linden, D.E.J., Goebel, R., & Muckli, L. (2006) The temporal characteristics of motion processing in hMT/V5+: combining fMRI and neuronavigated TMS. *NeuroImage*, *29*, 1326–1335.

Salzman, C. D., Britten, K. H., & Newsome, W. T. (1990) Cortical microstimulation influences perceptual judgements of motion direction. *Nature*, *346*, 174–177.

Salzman, C.D., Murasugi, C.M., Britten, K.H., & Newsome, W.T. (1992) Microstimulation in visual area MT: effects on direction discrimination performance. *Journal of Neuroscience*, *12*, 2331–2355.

Sanabria, D., Spence, S., & Soto-Faraco, S. (2007) Perceptual and decisional contributions to audiovisual interactions in the perception of apparent motion: a signal detection study. *Cognition*, *102*, 299–310.

Schiff, N.D., Giacino, J.T., Kalmar, K., Victor, J.D., Baker, K., Gerber, M., *et al.* (2007) Behavioural improvements with thalamic stimulation after severe traumatic brain injury. *Nature*, *448*, 600–604.

Schneeweis, D.M., & Schnapf, J.L. (1999) The photovoltage of macaque cone photoreceptors: adaptation, noise, and kinetics. *Journal of Neuroscience*, *19*, 1203–1216.

Schroeder, C.E., & Foxe, J.J. (2002) The timing and laminar profile of converging inputs to multisensory areas of the macaque neocortex. *Cognitive Brain Research*, *14*, 187–198.

Schurmann, M., Caetano, G., Hlushchuk, Y., Jousmaki, V., & Hari, R. (2006) Touch activates human auditory cortex. *NeuroImage*, *30*, 1325–1331.

Seetharaman, G., Lakhotia, A., & Blasch, E.P. (2006) Unmanned vehicles come of age: the DARPA grand challenge. *Computer*, *39*, 26–29.

Semple, M.N., & Scott, B.H. (2003) Cortical mechanisms in hearing. *Current Opinion in Neurobiology*, *13*, 167–173.

Shannon, C.E. (1948) A mathematical theory of communication. *The Bell System Technical Journal*, *27*, 379–423.

Sharpee, T.O., Sugihara, H., Kurgansky, A.V., Rebrik, S.P., Stryker, M.P., & Miller, K.D. (2006) Adaptive filtering enhances information transmission in visual cortex. *Nature*, *439*, 936–942.

Sillito, A., & Jones, H. (2002) Corticothalamic interactions in the transfer of visual information. *Philosophical Transactions of the Royal Society of London, B*, *357*, 1739–1752.

Sireteanu, R., Oertel, V., Mohr, H., Linden, D., & Singer, W. (2008) Graphical illustration and functional neuroimaging of visual hallucinations during prolonged blindfolding: a comparison of visual imagery. *Perception, 37*, 1805–1821.

Snowden, R.J., Stimpson, N., & Ruddle, R.A. (1998) Speed perception fogs up as visibility drops. *Nature, 392*, 450.

Spence, C., Levitan, C.A., Shankar, M.U., & Zampini, M. (2010) Does food color influence taste and flavour perception in humans? *Chemosensory Perception, 3*, 68–84.

Steinhauer, S.R., Siegle, G.J., Condray, R., & Pless, M. (2004) Sympathetic and parasympathetic innervation of pupillary dilation during sustained processing. *International Journal of Psychophysiology, 52*, 77–86.

Sterzer, P., & Kleinschmidt, A. (2007) A neural basis for inference in perceptual ambiguity. *Proceedings of the National Academy of Sciences, 104*, 323–328.

Stocker, A.A., & Simoncelli, E.P. (2006) Noise characteristics and prior expectations in human visual speed perception. *Nature Neuroscience, 9*, 578–585.

Stott, R. (2002) Interaction between the senses: vision and the vestibular system. In D. Roberts (ed.) *Signals and Perception* (pp. 355–364). Basingstoke, UK: Palgrave Macmillan.

Sutherland, N.S. (1961) Figural aftereffects and apparent size. *Quarterly Journal of Experimental Psychology, 13*, 222–228.

Tatler, B.W., Gilchrist, I.D., & Rusted, J. (2003) The time course of abstract visual representation. *Perception, 32*, 579–592.

Teghtsoonian, R. (1971) On the exponents in Steven's law and the constant in Ekman's law. *Psychological Review, 78*, 71–80.

Thompson, P. (1982) Perceived rate of movement depends on contrast. *Vision Research, 22*, 377–380.

Tolhurst, D.J., & Thompson, P.G. (1975) Orientation illusions and after-effects: inhibition between channels. *Vision Research, 15*, 967–972.

Tong, F., Meng, M., & Blake, R. (2006) Neural bases of binocular rivalry. *Trends in Cognitive Sciences, 10*, 502–511.

Tononi, G. (2004) An information integration theory of consciousness. *BMC Neuroscience, 5*(1), 42.

Tootell, R.B.H., Silverman, M., Switckes, E., & De Valois, R. (1982) Deoxyglucose analysis of retinotopic organization in primate striate cortex. *Science, 218*, 902–904.

Tootell, R.B.H., Reppas, J.B., Kwong, K.K., Malach, R., Born, R.T., Brady, T.J., *et al.* (1995) Functional analysis of human MT and related visual cortical areas using magnetic resonance imaging. *Journal of Neuroscience, 15*, 3215–3230.

Torebjork, H.E., & Ochoa, J.L. (1990) New method to identify nociceptor units innervating glabrous skin of the human hand. *Experimental Brain Research, 81*, 509–514.

Treisman, M. (1977) Motion sickness: an evolutionary hypothesis. *Science, 197*, 493–495.

Turing, A. (1936) On computable numbers with an application to the Entscheidungsproblem. *Proceedings of the London Mathematical Society, 42*, 230–265.

Ullman, S. (1984) Maximising rigidity: the incremental recovery of 3-D stucture from rigid and nonrigid motion. *Perception, 13*, 255–274.

Ungerleider, L.G., & Mishkin, M. (1982) Two cortical visual systems. In D.J. Ingle, M.A. Goodale, & R.J.W. Mansfield (eds) *Analysis of Visual Behavior* (pp. 549–586). Cambridge, MA: MIT Press.

von Melchner, L., Pallas, S.L., & Sur, M. (2000) Visual behaviour mediated by retinal projections directed to the auditory pathway. *Nature, 404*, 871–876.

Ward, J. (2008) *Synesthesia*. Hove, UK: Psychology Press.

Ward, J., & Meijer, P. (2010) Visual experiences in the blind induced by an auditory sensory substitution device. *Consciousness and Cognition, 19*, 492–500.

Wark, B., Lundstrom, B.N., & Fairhall, A. (2007) Sensory adaptation. *Current Opinion in Neurobiology, 17*, 423–429.

Watanabe, K., & Shimojo, S. (2001) When sound affects vision: effects of auditory grouping on visual motion perception. *Psychological Science, 12*, 109–116.

Weinstein, S. (1968) Intensive and extensive aspects of tactile sensitivity as a function of body part, sex, and laterality. In D. Kenshalo (ed.) *The Skin Senses* (pp. 195–222). Springfield, IL: Thomas.

Weiss, Y., Simoncelli, E.P., & Adelson, E.H. (2002) Motion illusions as optimal percepts. *Nature Neuroscience, 5*, 598–604.

Wenger, D.M. (2003) The mind's best trick: how we experience conscious free will. *Trends in Cognitive Sciences, 7*, 65–69.

White, N.S., & Alkire, M.T. (2003) Impaired thalamocortical connectivity in humans during general-anesthesic-induced unconsciousness. *NeuroImage, 19*, 402–411.

Wilson, A.D., & Baietto, M. (2009) Applications and advances in electronic-nose technologies. *Sensors, 9*, 5099–5148.

Wolfe, J.M., Kluender, K.R., Levi, D.M., Bartoshuk, L.M., Herz, R.S., Klatsky, R.L., *et al.* (2006) *Sensation and Perception*. Sunderland, MA: Sinauer.

Wuerger, S.M., Hofbauer, M., & Meyer, G.F. (2003) The integration of auditory and visual motion signals at threshold. *Perception and Psychophysics, 65*, 1188–1196.

Yaro, C., & Ward, J. (2007) Searching for Shereshevskii: what is superior about the memory of synaesthetes? *Quarterly Journal of Experimental Psychology, 60*, 682–696.

Zeki, S. (1990) A century of cerebral achromatopsia. *Brain, 113*, 1721–1777.

Zellner, D.A., & Kautz, M.A. (1990) Color affects perceived odor intensity. *Journal of Experimental Psychology: Human Perception and Performance, 16*, 391–397.

Zhou, W., & Chen, D. (2009) Binaral rivalry between the nostrils and in the cortex. *Current Biology, 19*, 1561–1565.

Zihl, J., Von Cramon, D., & Mai, N. (1983) Selective disturbance of movement vision after bilateral brain damage. *Brain, 106*, 313–340.

Zubek, J.P. (1964) Effects of prolonged sensory and perceptual deprivation. *British Medical Bulletin, 20*, 38–42.

Author index

Subject index

Page numbers in **bold** indicate key term definitions.